Disney LEARNING

MATH
BRAIN BOOST

GRADE
1

NELSON

This workbook belongs to:

Disney LEARNING

COPYRIGHT © 2018 Disney Enterprises, Inc.
All rights reserved.

Pixar properties © Disney/Pixar

Published by Nelson Education Ltd.

ISBN-13: 978-0-17-685500-0
ISBN-10: 0-17-685500-9

Printed and bound in Canada
1 2 3 4   21 20 19 18

For more information contact Nelson Education Ltd.,
1120 Birchmount Road, Toronto, Ontario M1K 5G4.
Or you can visit our website at nelson.com.

For permission to use material from this text or product,
submit all requests online at cengage.com/permissions.
Further questions about permissions can be emailed to
permissionrequest@cengage.com.

Credits: 26, 27, 46, 47: Coin images © 2018 Royal Canadian Mint.

Contents

Track Your Learning

START

1 2 3 4 5

21 20 19 18 17 16

22 23 24 25 26 27

45 44 43 42 41 40 39

46 47 48 49 50 51

69 68 67 66 65

70 71 72 73 74

Colour a circle for every completed activity
to finish the Brain Boost learning path!

Picture Search

Ariel loves to swim!

Read each sentence. Trace each number. Search the image for the objects mentioned in each sentence. Count those objects in the image.

Ariel has 1 tail.

She has 2 eyes.

There are 3 fish with brown stripes.

The octopus is playing on 4 clamshell drums.

The little lobster is playing 5 green drums.

6 jellyfish are enjoying the music.

There are 7 fish altogether.

8 seahorses swim under Ariel.

9 green bubbles float near Sebastian.

10 flowers grow on the ocean floor.

Matching

There are lots of fish in the sea! Print the numbers and words. Then draw a line to match the number to the word.

1	four
2	two
3	five
4	one
5	three

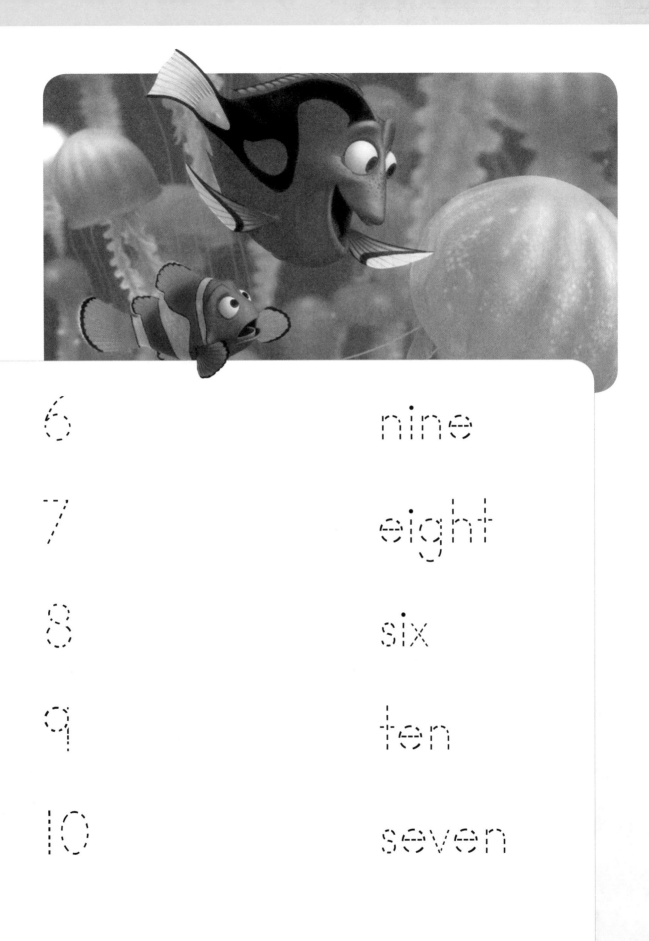

6   nine

7   eight

8   six

9   ten

10   seven

Colour to Complete

Who is chasing Ariel and Flounder? To find out, colour the picture. Use the Colour Key.

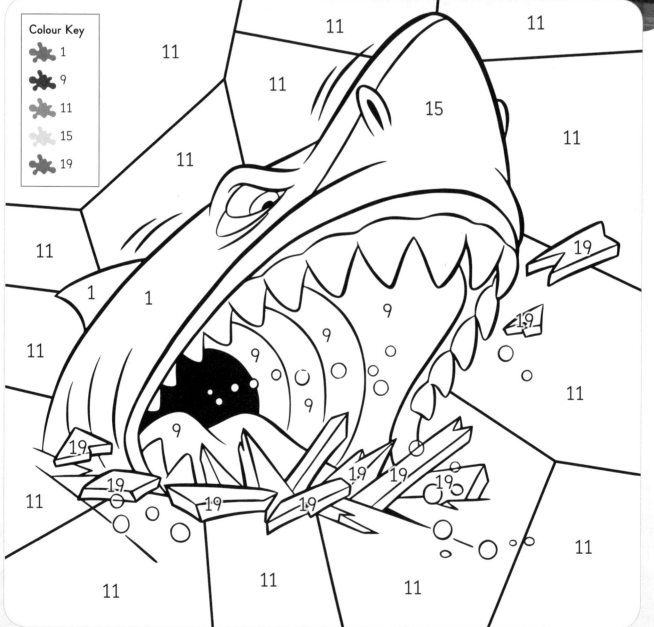

Colour Key

1

9

11

15

19

Crack the Code

What does Ariel love to do? To find out, spell each number. Use the boxed letters to crack the code! The first one is done for you.

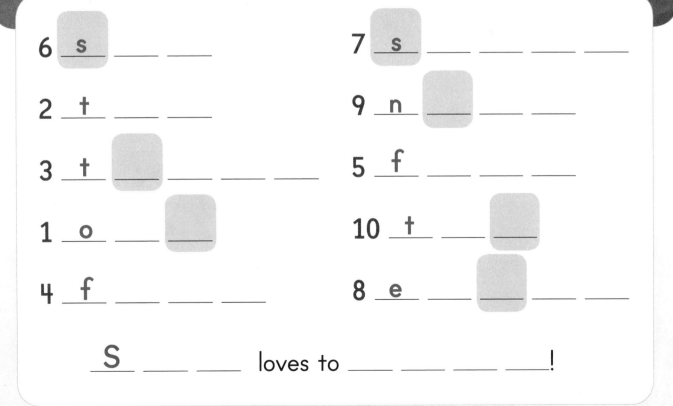

6 s __ __ __

2 t __ __ __

3 t __ __ __ __ __

1 o __ __ __

4 f __ __ __

7 s __ __ __ __ __

9 n __ __ __

5 f __ __ __

10 t __ __ __

8 e __ __ __ __

__ S __ __ __ loves to __ __ __ __ !

Matching

Marlin sees many groups of animals when he searches for Nemo.

Count how many are in each group. Match each group of objects to the correct number.

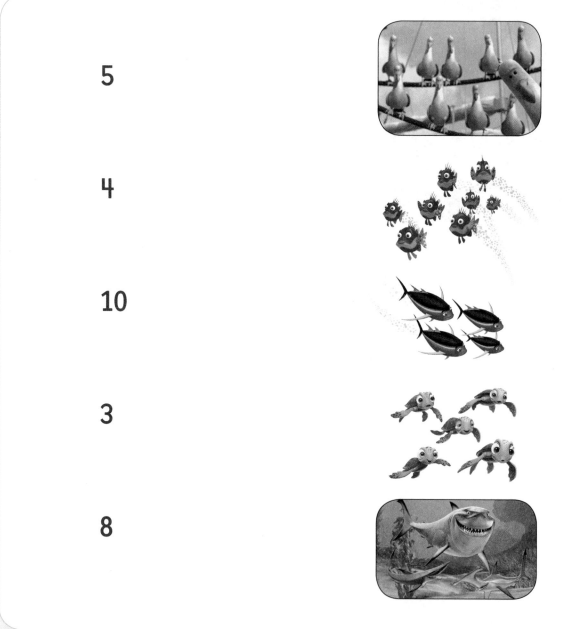

5

4

10

3

8

Word Search

Nemo has 6 friends.
6 can also be shown
using the word **six**.

(Circle) the number words
below in the word search.

E	I	G	H	T	O	Z	R		ONE
F	O	U	R	V	T	E	N		TWO
L	N	I	N	E	J	B	Z		THREE
S	I	X	U	Q	V	Q	B		FOUR
O	N	E	F	F	I	V	E		FIVE
I	B	T	S	E	V	E	N		SIX
G	A	Z	T	W	O	H	S		SEVEN
T	A	T	H	R	E	E	B		EIGHT
									NINE
									TEN

HINT Look for words that read across.

Fill In the Blanks

How many pearls are under the sea? Count the number of pearls in each set. Trace the number.

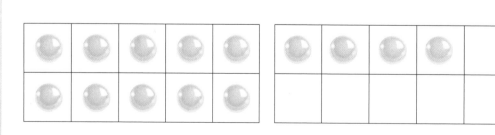

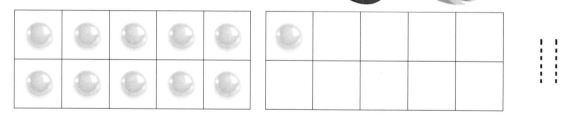

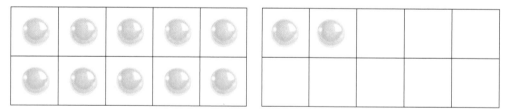

11

12

13

14

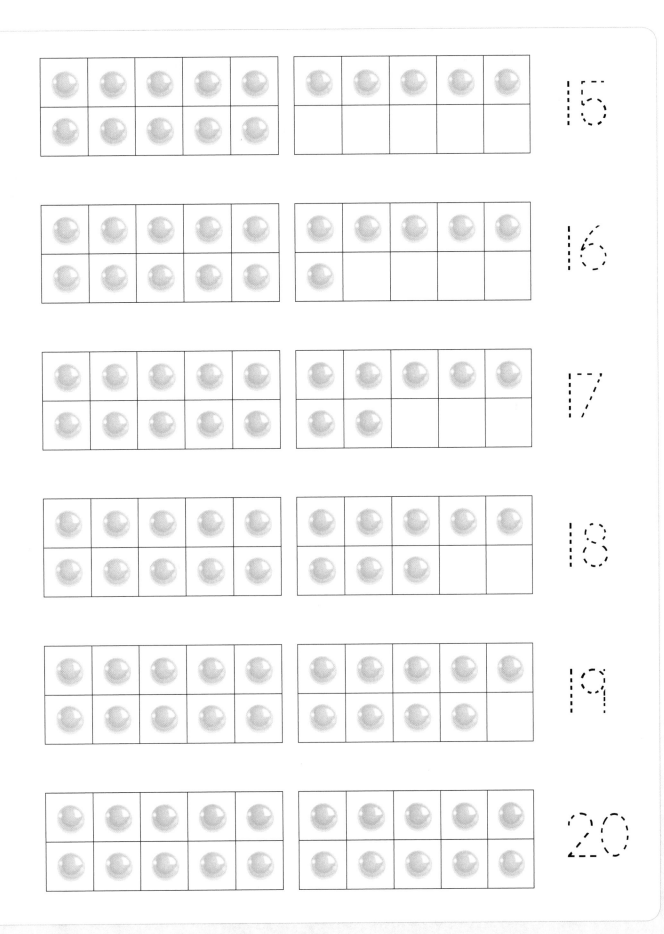

15

16

17

18

19

20

Word Search

There are 11 seagulls. 11 can be shown using the word **eleven**. Circle the number words in the word search.

```
F  T  H  I  R  T  E  E  N  N
R  O  F  I  F  T  E  E  N  B
P  U  N  I  N  E  T  E  E  N
T  K  H  T  W  E  L  V  E  A
T  W  E  N  T  Y  S  D  I  W
J  S  I  X  T  E  E  N  N  F
Q  O  E  I  G  H  T  E  E  N
F  O  U  R  T  E  E  N  B  W
E  L  E  V  E  N  Y  R  T  A
S  E  V  E  N  T  E  E  N  S
```

ELEVEN   TWELVE   THIRTEEN   FOURTEEN

FIFTEEN   SIXTEEN   SEVENTEEN

EIGHTEEN   NINETEEN   TWENTY

HINT Look for words that read across.

Fill In the Blanks

Lots of turtles ride on the East Australian Current.

Write the word for each numeral.

11 _____   12 _____

13 _____   14 _____

15 _____   16 _____

17 _____   18 _____

19 _____   20 _____

HINT Check page 14 for the correct spelling of each word.

Fill In the Blanks

King Triton's trident is missing!

Fill in the missing numbers in each set.

1 _____ 3 _____ _____ 6

_____ _____ 9 10

11 _____ 13 _____ 15

_____ 17 _____ 19 _____

Ariel is losing her voice!
Fill in the missing numbers
in each set. You will need
to count backward.

20 _____ 18 _____ 16 15

14 13 _____ _____ 10

9 _____ 7 _____

5 _____ 3 2 _____

HINT Use the 100-chart on page 111
to help you count backward.

17

Crack the Code

Who is Marlin looking for? To find out, draw a circle around the set that has less. Use the letter beside that set to crack the code.

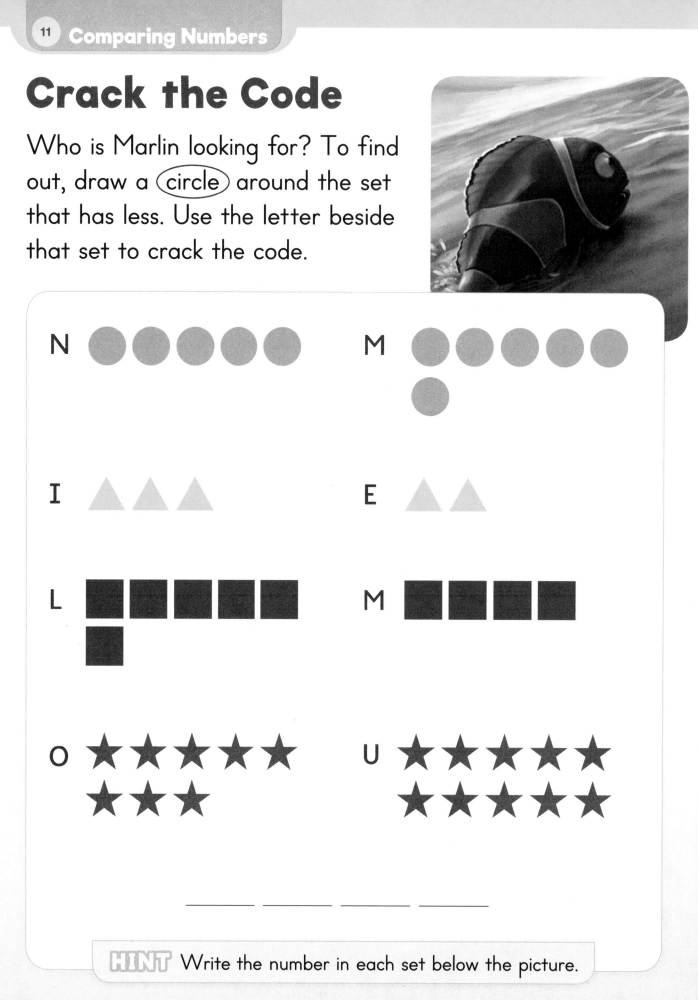

N ● ● ● ● ●

M ● ● ● ● ●
  ●

I ▲ ▲ ▲

E ▲ ▲

L ■ ■ ■ ■ ■
  ■

M ■ ■ ■ ■

O ★ ★ ★ ★ ★
  ★ ★ ★

U ★ ★ ★ ★ ★
  ★ ★ ★ ★ ★

____ ____ ____ ____

HINT Write the number in each set below the picture.

18

Colour to Complete

Circle the larger number in each fish. Use the Colour Key to colour the fish.

Colour Key

🔵 14   🔵 15   🔵 18   🔵 20

14   4

13   15

18   8

2   20

Picture Search

Try to estimate how many friends have gathered to welcome Nemo back!
How many animals are in each picture?

I estimate there are about _____ animals.

I estimate there are

about _____ animals.

I estimate there are

about _____ animals.

I estimate there are

about _____ animals.

I estimate there are

about _____ fish eyes.

Fill In the Blanks

Many animals live in the sea.

Estimate how many animals are in each set. Then count them to check your estimate.

I estimate there are about _____ dolphins.

There are _____ dolphins.

I estimate there are about _____ seahorses.

There are _____ seahorses.

I estimate there are about _____ fish.

There are _____ fish.

HINT It is great when your estimate is close to the actual number, but it is all right for your estimate to not be the actual number!

Picture Search

Prince Eric likes to sail the ocean and see lots of creatures!

Estimate how many squid are in this array. Then count them to check your estimate.

I estimate there are about _____ squid.

There are _____ squid.

Was your estimate close to the number you counted?

_____

HINT Look at the number of squid in each group to help you guess more accurately.

Fill In the Blanks

How many merpeople are swimming in the sea? Estimate how many. Then count.

I estimate that there are about _____ merpeople swimming in the sea.

I count _____ merpeople swimming in the sea.

Look at the image again. Now estimate how many fish there are.

I estimate that there are about _____ fish swimming in the sea.

I count _____ fish swimming in the sea.

How many shells are in each set?
Estimate the number. Then count.

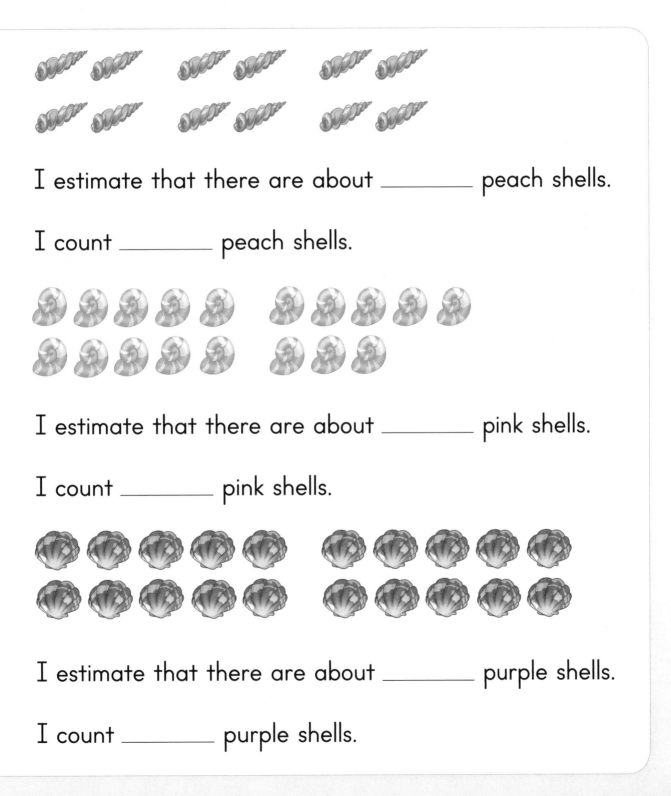

I estimate that there are about _____ peach shells.

I count _____ peach shells.

I estimate that there are about _____ pink shells.

I count _____ pink shells.

I estimate that there are about _____ purple shells.

I count _____ purple shells.

Matching

Bubbles waits beside the treasure chest. How much money might the chest hold?

Draw a line to match each coin to its correct value.

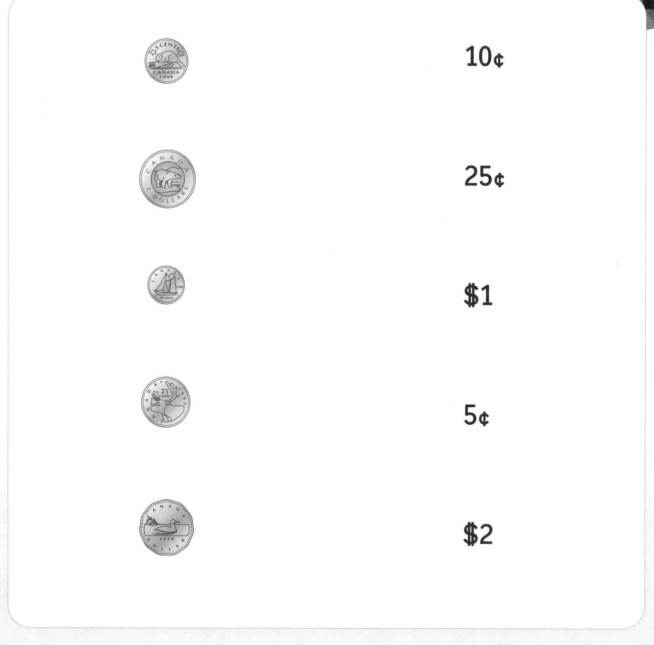

10¢

25¢

$1

5¢

$2

Maze

Dr. Sherman spends money to care for his fish.

Start with the coin with the lowest value. Make your way to the coin with the highest value.

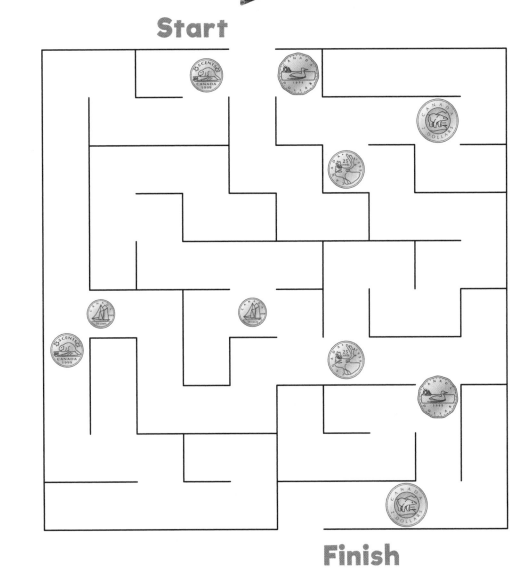

Start

Finish

Picture Search

Ariel and her friends are lining up to dance.
Ariel is first in line.

Draw a box around the second friend in line.

Circle the third friend in the line.

Underline the fourth friend in line.

Matching

Ariel sees her toes for the first time!

Draw a line to match the ordinal number and the ordinal word.

4th	third
2nd	fourth
5th	first
3rd	fifth
1st	second

Maze

Dory and Marlin are trying to swim away from Bruce! Count forward from 1 to 20 through the maze.

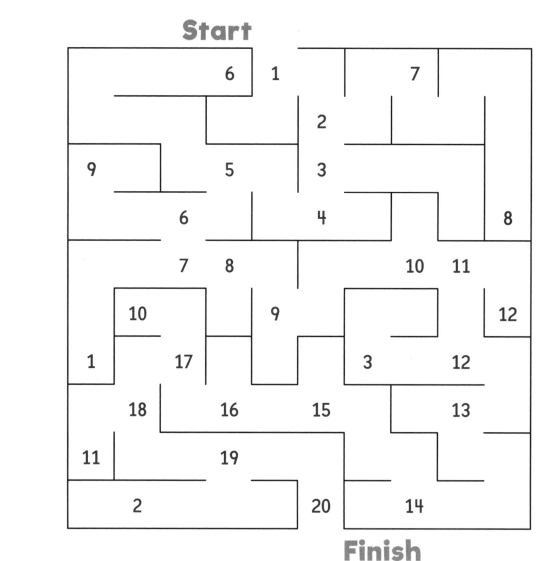

Start

Finish

HINT If you have not followed numbers in order, you are on the wrong path.

Connect the Dots

What does Dory drop into the trench? To find out, connect the dots. Count backward from 20 to 1.

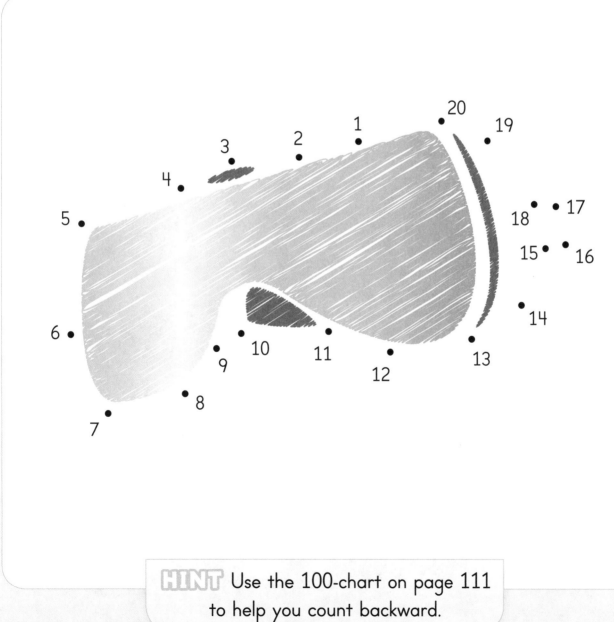

HINT Use the 100-chart on page 111 to help you count backward.

31

Matching

Chef Louis needs many different ingredients for his soups. The number of ingredients he needs for each soup can be shown using blocks.

Match each group of blocks with the number it represents.

13

18

3

7

9

HINT You can skip count by 5s.

Connect the Dots

Ursula has two eels to help her, Flotsam and Jetsam. Skip count by 2s from 2 to 50 to complete the image.

HINT Use the 100-chart on page 111 to help you skip count.

33

Maze

How will Marlin get through the East Australian Current? With the help of Crush and Squirt and you! Find your way through the maze. Skip count by 5s from 5 to 75.

Start

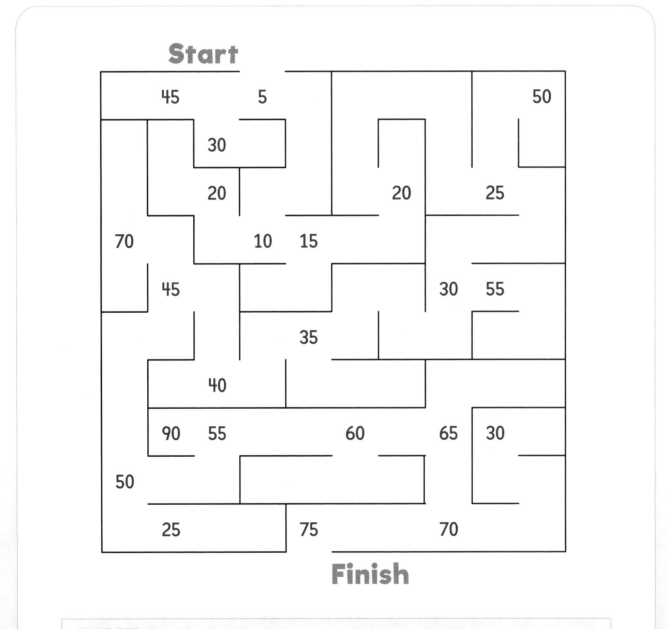

45	5		50
30			
20		20	25
70	10 15		
45		30	55
	35		
40			
90 55	60	65	30
50			
25	75	70	

Finish

HINT Use the 100-chart on page 111 to help you skip count.

34

Connect the Dots

There are too many jellyfish in Marlin's way! To find the path, connect the dots by skip counting by 10s.

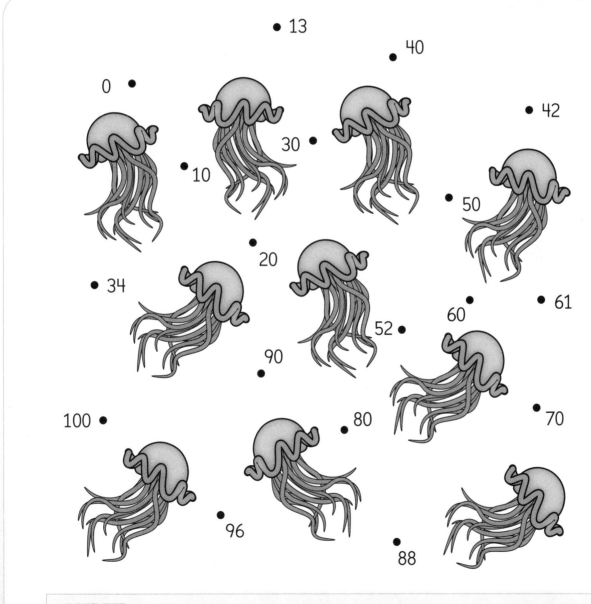

• 13

• 40

0 •

• 42

30 •

10 •

• 50

• 34

20 •

• 61

60 •

52 •

90 •

100 •

• 80

• 70

96 •

88 •

HINT Use the 100-chart on page 111 to help you skip count.

Matching

Ursula has six tentacles. You can show 6 like this or like this . Match the groups of blocks that are equal.

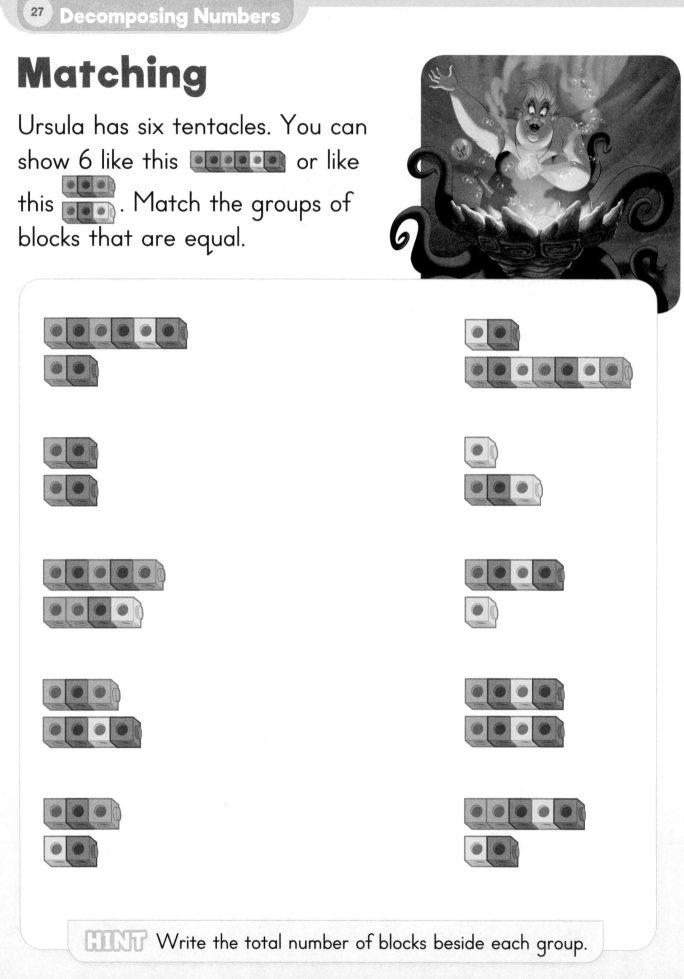

HINT Write the total number of blocks beside each group.

Colour to Complete

Seven fish wait for Sebastian to come up with a new song. You can show 7 in different ways.

$1 + 6 = 7$ $2 + 5 = 7$ $3 + 4 = 7$

Determine the sum beside each fish. Use the sum and the Colour Key to colour the fish.

2 + 3 =

4 + 4 =

3 + 7 =

5 + 5 =

1 + 4 =

1 + 9 =

2 + 6 =

Colour Key
5   8   10

HINT Use counters to represent the numbers on each fish.

Fill In the Blanks

3 birds are flying. 2 birds sit on the rock. There are 5 birds altogether.

$3 + 2 = 5$

Write the addition sentence for each set.

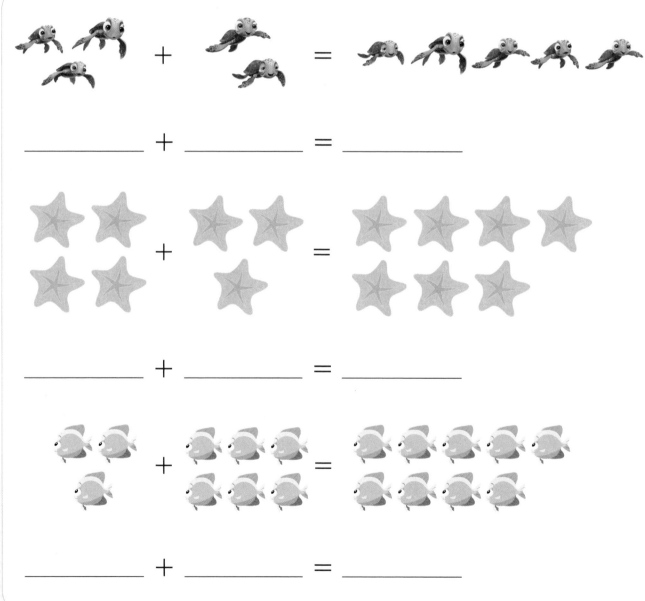

_____ + _____ = _____

_____ + _____ = _____

_____ + _____ = _____

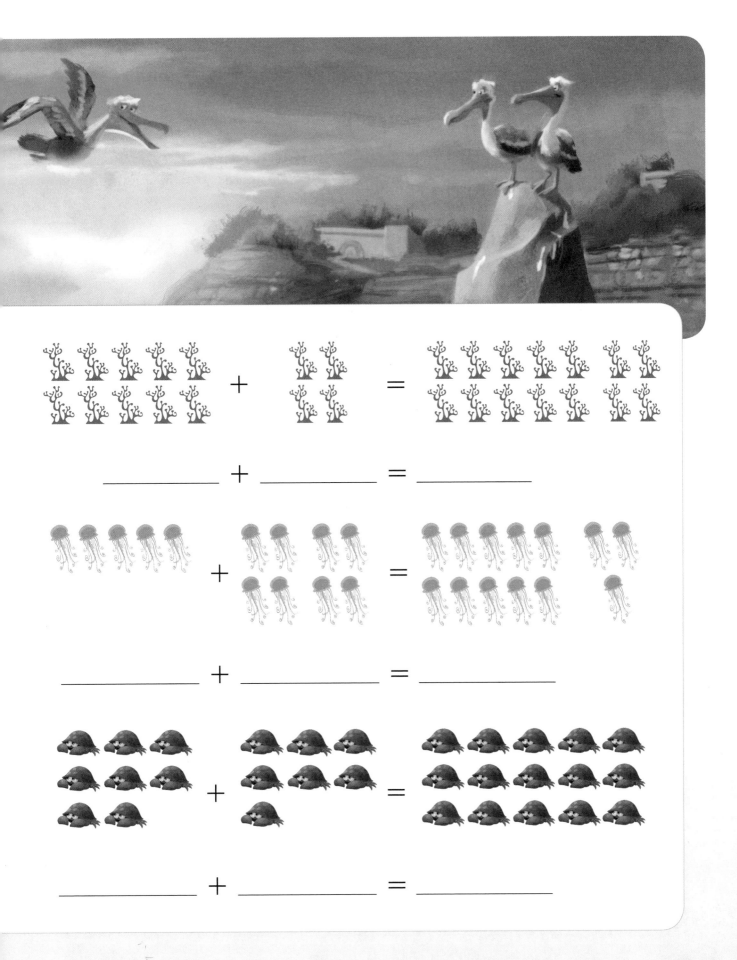

_____ + _____ = _____

_____ + _____ = _____

_____ + _____ = _____

Crack the Code

What does King Triton create after Ariel and Eric's wedding? To find out, add the numbers to solve each sum. Use the letter beside each sum to crack the code.

$$4 + 4$$
B

$$5 + 5$$
A

$$7 + 7$$
N

$$6 + 6$$
O

$$10 + 10$$
R

$$8 + 8$$
W

$$9 + 9$$
I

$$3 + 3$$
S

___ ___ ___ ___ ___ ___ ___ ___
10   20   10   18   14   8   12   16

Fill In the Blanks

Chef Louis made 6 cakes for Ariel's wedding. 5 cakes were eaten. How many cakes are left?

$6 - 5 = 1$

Write the subtraction sentence for each set. The first one is done for you.

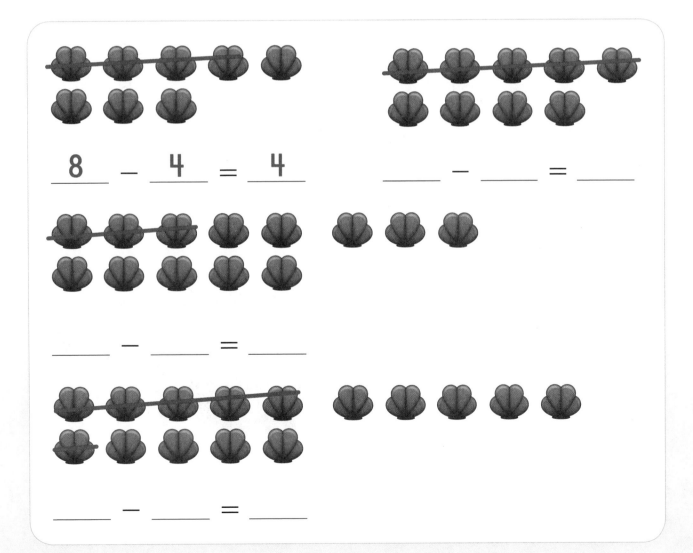

$\underline{\quad 8 \quad} - \underline{\quad 4 \quad} = \underline{\quad 4 \quad}$ $\underline{\qquad} - \underline{\qquad} = \underline{\qquad}$

$\underline{\qquad} - \underline{\qquad} = \underline{\qquad}$

$\underline{\qquad} - \underline{\qquad} = \underline{\qquad}$

Crack the Code

Who is the funniest fish in the ocean? To find out, subtract the numbers to solve each difference. Then crack the code!

5	9	3	18
− 1	− 6	− 3	− 6
S	N	F	W

10	8	4	15
− 4	− 3	− 2	− 5
C	I	L	O

7	14
− 6	− 3
A	H

$\overline{\hphantom{xxx}}$ $\overline{\hphantom{xxx}}$ $\overline{\hphantom{xxx}}$ $\overline{\hphantom{xxx}}$ $\overline{\hphantom{xxx}}$ $\overline{\hphantom{xxx}}$
1   6   2   10   12   3

$\overline{\hphantom{xxx}}$ $\overline{\hphantom{xxx}}$ $\overline{\hphantom{xxx}}$ $\overline{\hphantom{xxx}}$
0   5   4   11

Maze

Help Ariel rescue Eric! Find your way through the maze. The correct path has sums that are even numbers.

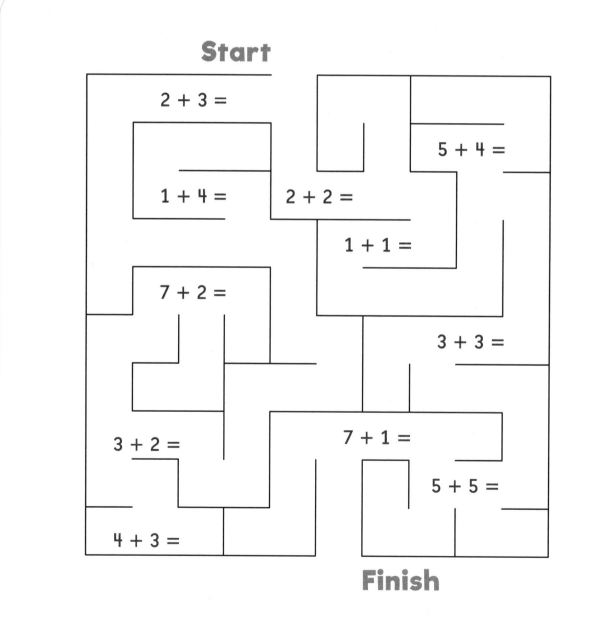

Start

2 + 3 =

5 + 4 =

1 + 4 =   2 + 2 =

1 + 1 =

7 + 2 =

3 + 3 =

3 + 2 =   7 + 1 =

5 + 5 =

4 + 3 =

Finish

HINT Even numbers end in 0, 2, 4, 6, or 8.

Colour to Complete

Ursula's eels have tipped the boat.
2 people were in the boat.
2 people fell out. Now 0 people
are in the boat.

$2 - 2 = 0$

Calculate each difference. Use the
Colour Key to colour the picture.

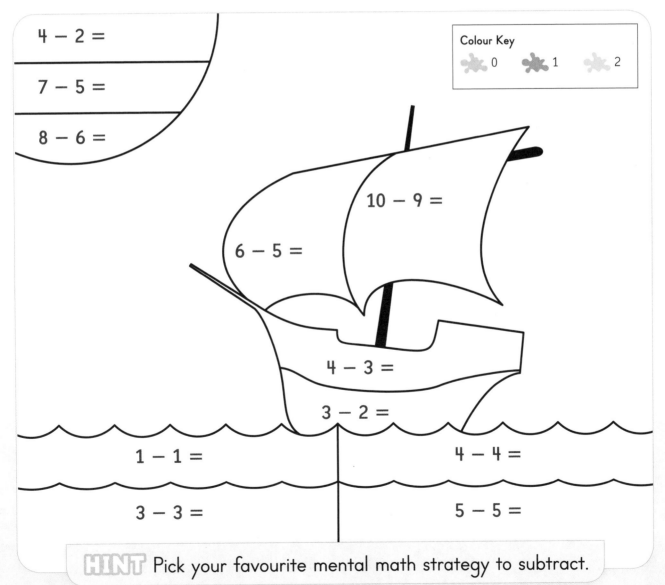

$4 - 2 =$

$7 - 5 =$

$8 - 6 =$

Colour Key

0   1   2

$10 - 9 =$

$6 - 5 =$

$4 - 3 =$

$3 - 2 =$

$1 - 1 =$

$4 - 4 =$

$3 - 3 =$

$5 - 5 =$

HINT Pick your favourite mental math strategy to subtract.

Matching

A treasure chest is full of money! Add up the coins in each treasure chest. Match each chest to the correct amount. The first one has been done for you.

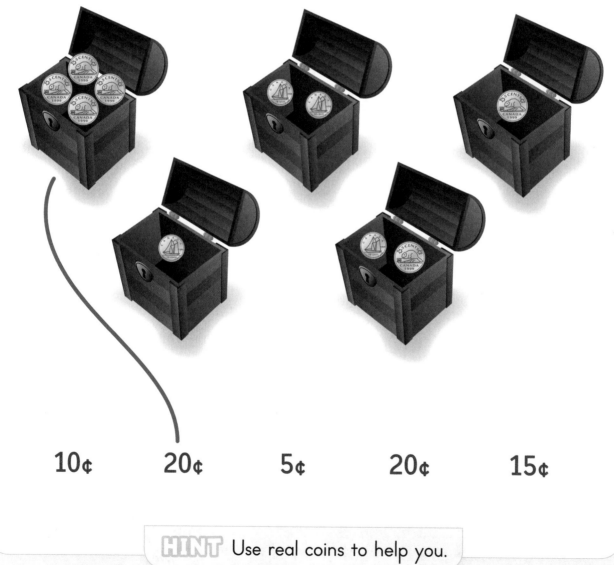

10¢   20¢   5¢   20¢   15¢

HINT Use real coins to help you.

Fill In the Blanks

Dr. Sherman spends money on a new filter for the fish tank. He has to know how to subtract using coins. Write a subtraction sentence for each set of coins.

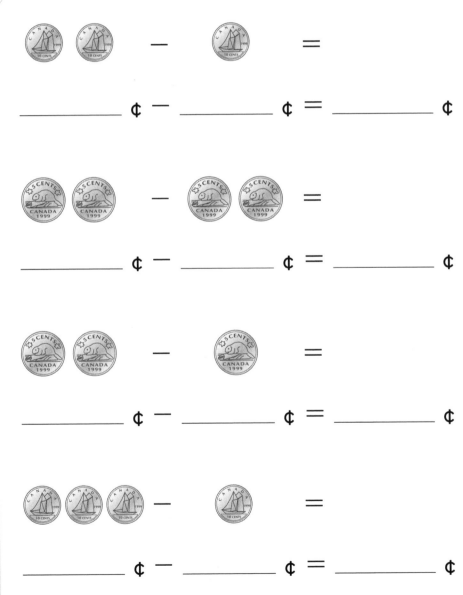

_____ ¢ — _____ ¢ = _____ ¢

_____ ¢ — _____ ¢ = _____ ¢

_____ ¢ — _____ ¢ = _____ ¢

_____ ¢ — _____ ¢ = _____ ¢

Matching

Ariel swims in the ocean. She has many living things around her. Sort the living things.

Draw a line from each fish to the box labelled **Fish**. The first one is done for you.

Draw a line from each flower to the box labelled **Flowers**.

Fish

Flowers

Picture Search

Ariel's friends sing to her and Prince Eric.

Examine the image. Sort the friends into groups.

Write the number **1** on all the animals that have fins.

Write the number **2** on all the animals that have beaks.

Write the number **3** on all the animals that have shells.

Matching

There are many patterns under the sea. For each pattern, draw a line to the image that comes next.

HINT Say the word for each image.
Think about what comes next.

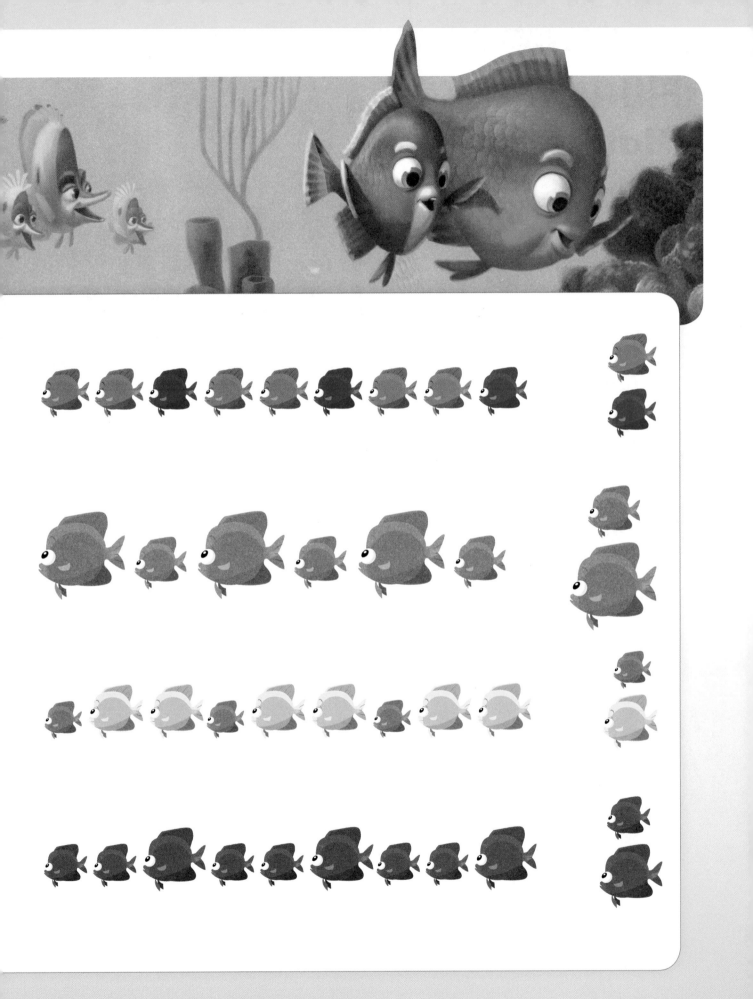

Fill In the Blanks

Sebastian uses a pattern to conduct the fish as they play their instruments.

Fill in each blank to extend each pattern.

XYXYXY＿＿＿＿＿

HAAHAAHAA＿＿＿＿＿＿＿＿

1 1 5 1 1 5 1 1 5 _____ _____ _____

 _____ _____ _____

u U u U u U u _____ _____

 _____ _____

Colour to Complete

Make your own patterns using the shapes below.

Colour the first star blue. Colour the second star yellow. Complete the pattern.

☆☆☆☆☆☆☆☆

Colour the first triangle red. Colour the second triangle blue. Colour the third triangle blue. Complete the pattern.

Colour the first circle red. Colour the second circle red. Colour the third circle green. Complete the pattern.

○○○○○○○○○○

Choose two colours to make a pattern.

Choose three colours to make a pattern.

Use triangles to create a pattern that changes by size.

Create your own pattern! Draw your pattern below.

HINT Shapes in a pattern can change by colour, shape, size, direction, or number.

Solve the Riddles

Ariel enjoys looking for treasure. These riddles will help you solve the missing numbers.

1. I am a number less than 8 and greater than 6.

   _____

2. I am a number less than 14 and greater than 12.

   _____

3. I am the number that comes right after 9.

   _____

4. I am the number that comes right before 16.

   _____

5. I am a number less than 3 and greater than 1.

   _____

HINT You can use a number line from 0 to 20 to help you solve the riddles.

Puzzle Pieces

Look at each set of puzzle pieces.

Draw a line to match the puzzle pieces. The number on the left should be less than the number on the right. The first one is done for you.

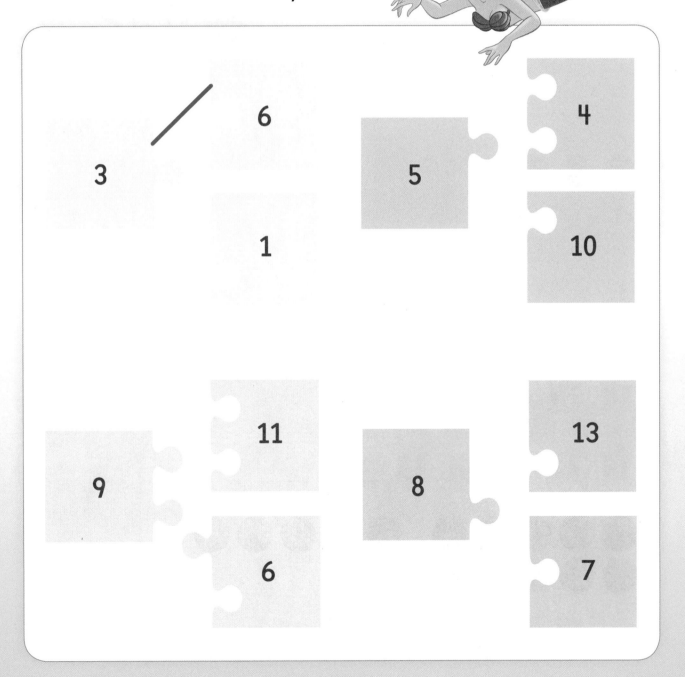

Fill In the Blanks

Chef Louis wants to add more items to his kitchen, including more crabs!

Write down a number that is greater than the number of items shown in each row.

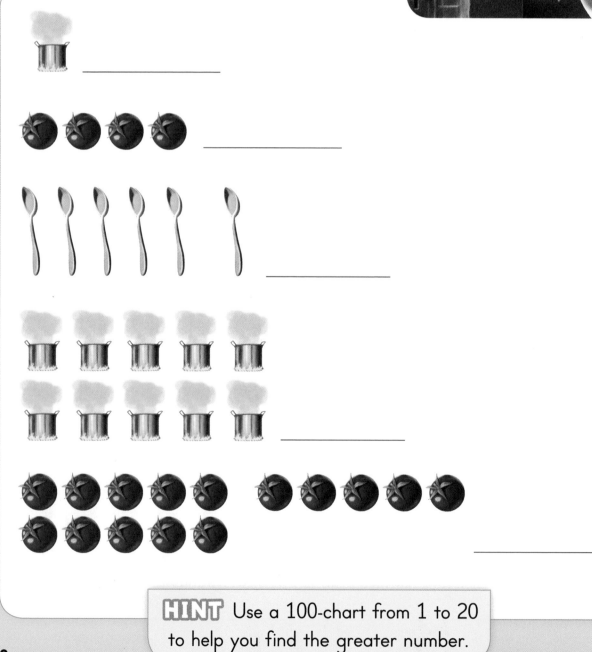

HINT Use a 100-chart from 1 to 20 to help you find the greater number.

Colour to Complete

Ariel, Sebastian, and Flounder enjoy spending time together under the sea!

Colour the greater number in each pair of shells.

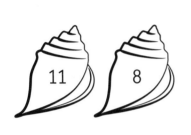  

11 8   7 5   5 11

  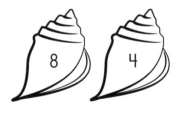

1 8   10 15   8 4

12 6   14 15   3 11

Crack the Code

What is the name of Dr. Sherman's niece? To find out, (circle) the bigger shape. Use the letter beside the bigger shape to crack the code!

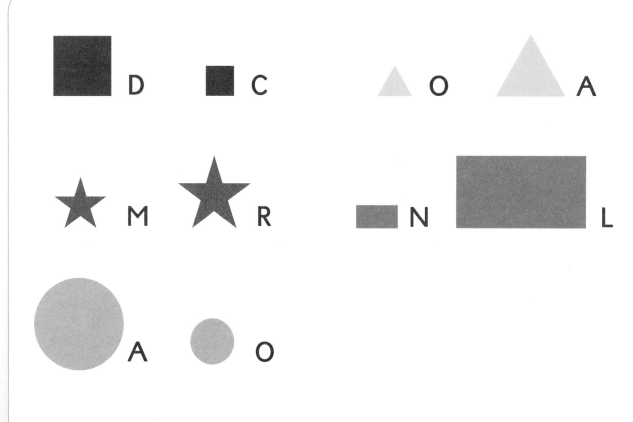

Place the letters here to spell her name:

_____ _____ _____ _____ _____

When Dr. Sherman gives Nemo to his niece, what does she do to the bag? To find out, (circle) the smaller shape. Use the letter beside the smaller shape to crack the code!

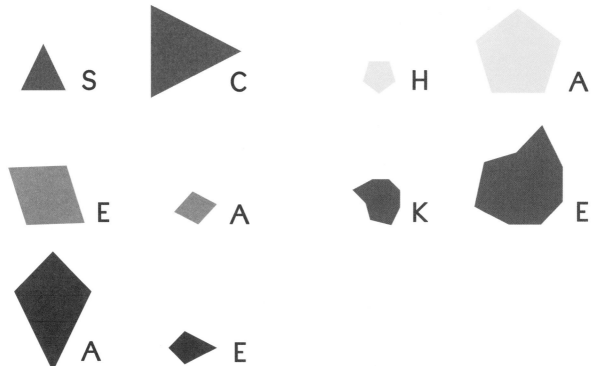

S   C   H   A

E   A   K   E

A   E

Place the letters here to spell the answer:

_____ _____ _____ _____ _____ IT!

Picture Search

Ariel is carrying a lot of heavy stuff.

Examine each pair of objects. Which object do you think is heavier? (Circle) that object.

HINT Think about the size of the object, but also about what it is made of. Is the heavier object always bigger?

Out of Order

Scuttle is holding some heavy objects!

Order the objects by their mass,
from lightest to heaviest.
Which object is the lightest?
Write the number 1 beside it.
Which object is the heaviest?
Write the number 3 beside it.

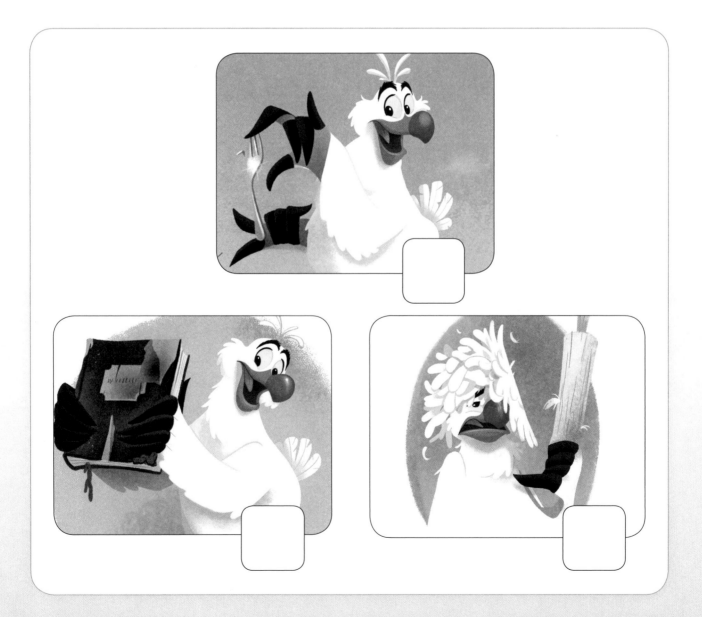

Picture Search

The fish tank holds a lot of water! Darla is holding a bag of water with a fish in it. There is very little water in that bag! The fish tank holds a lot more water than the bag.

Examine each pair of objects. (Circle) the object that can hold more water.

Out of Order

Each of these bags holds a different amount of water.

Which fish tank do you think can hold the least amount of water? Write the number 1 under it. Order the fish tanks by how much water they can hold, from least to greatest.

_____   _____   _____

HINT The number 3 goes below the fish tank that can hold the greatest amount of water.

Fill In the Blanks

King Triton is holding a long trident. The trident is longer than the spikes on his crown.

Count the paperclips to measure the length of each object. Write the length of each object.

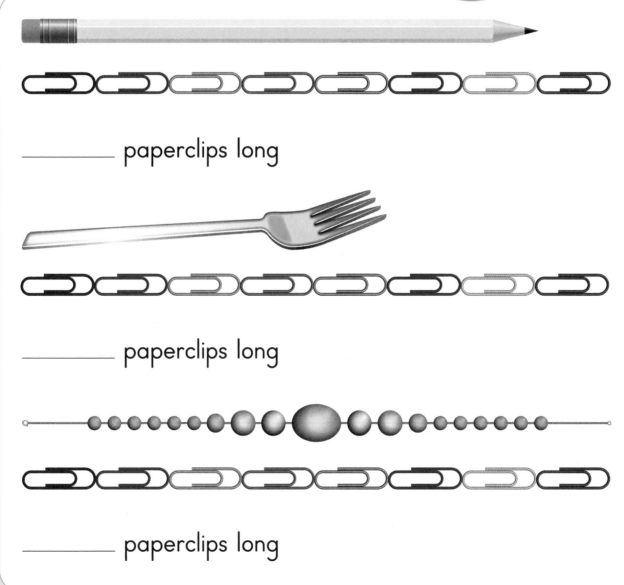

_____ paperclips long

_____ paperclips long

_____ paperclips long

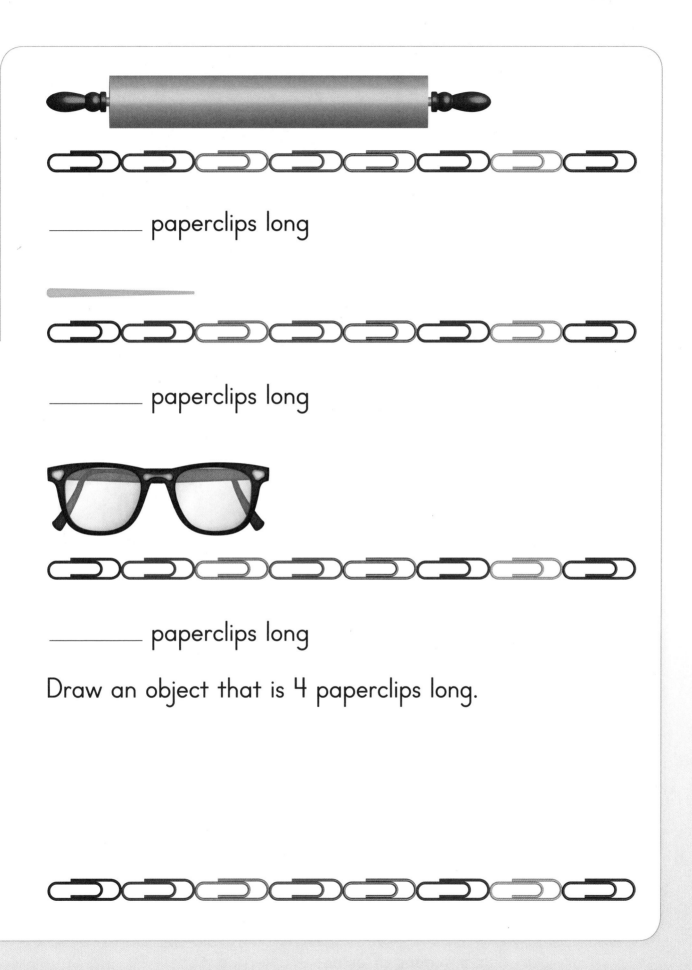

_____ paperclips long

_____ paperclips long

_____ paperclips long

Draw an object that is 4 paperclips long.

Matching

The Tank Gang race against the clock to get the tank dirty.

Match each activity to the correct time.

wake up

12:00 AM •PM

lunch

8:00 AM •PM

school
day ends

3:30 AM •PM

bedtime

7:00 •AM PM

HINT **a.m.** means before noon (morning).
p.m. means after noon (afternoon).

Solve the Riddles

Nemo has run out of time!
Dr. Sherman scoops him up.

Solve each riddle to figure out what time it is. Draw each time on a clock.

Half an hour past 1:00

Half an hour before 3:00

2 hours after 4:00

2 hours before 12:00

HINT The long hand shows the minutes.
The short hand shows the hours.

Matching

Scuttle is looking for his watch.

Can you tell what time it is? Match the clocks that show the same time.

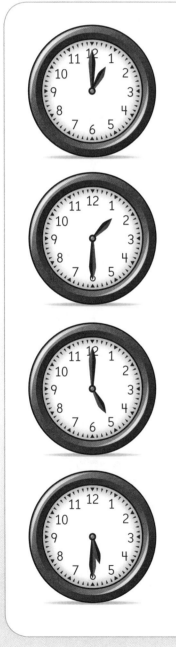

Out of Order

Ariel has a clock in her grotto. Its hands are missing. No wonder she loses track of time!

These clocks do not have hands. They are all out of order. Order the clocks, starting with the earliest time.

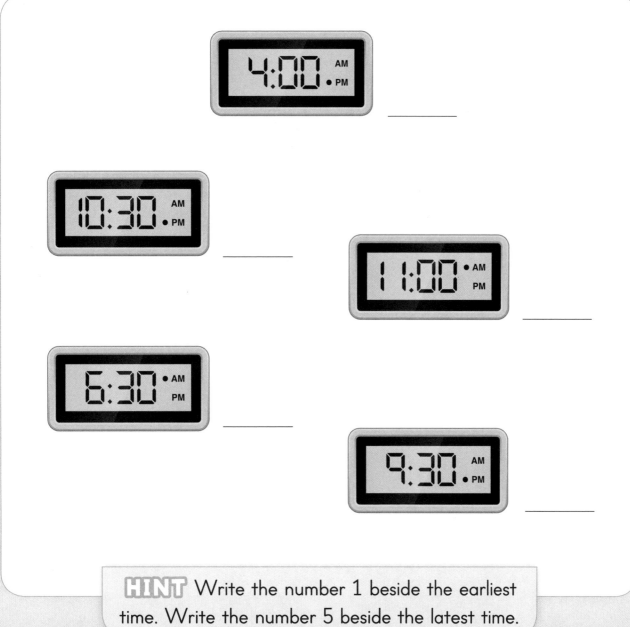

4:00 AM • PM _____

10:30 AM • PM _____

11:00 • AM PM _____

6:30 • AM PM _____

9:30 AM • PM _____

HINT Write the number 1 beside the earliest time. Write the number 5 beside the latest time.

Maze

The moon is shaped like a circle. Follow the circles to get through the maze.

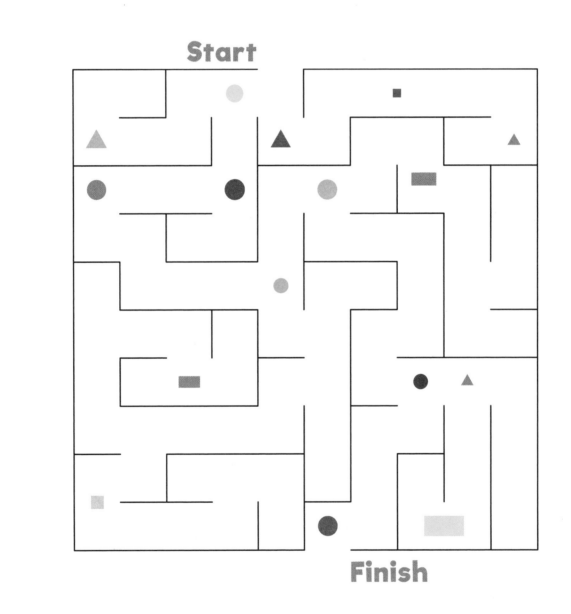

Start

Finish

Matching

Some of Bruce's teeth are shaped like triangles. Triangles have three sides.

Draw a line to match each 2-D shape with its name.

diamond

circle

rectangle

triangle

star

square

Word Search

There are different shapes on Ariel's luggage.

(Circle) the name of each shape in the word search.

```
W  A  V  X  I  B  W  A  N  H
J  V  I  Z  O  O  V  A  L  L
Z  B  S  A  D  P  I  N  N  B
V  C  I  R  C  L  E  S  Q  H
Z  S  T  R  I  A  N  G  L  E
J  U  L  T  L  H  A  S  C  D
R  E  C  T  A  N  G  L  E  Q
Z  C  S  Y  K  S  S  T  A  R
C  T  C  D  I  A  M  O  N  D
I  S  Q  U  A  R  E  G  S  C
```

CIRCLE   SQUARE   RECTANGLE

TRIANGLE   OVAL   STAR   DIAMOND

Solve the Riddles

Vanessa is looking in a mirror. The mirror is shaped like an oval. Scuttle is looking into a window. The window is shaped like a circle.

Solve each riddle to discover the shape.

1. I am perfectly round and have no corners.

   What am I? ____ ____ ____ ____ ____

2. I have four sides. Every side is the same length.

   What am I? ____ ____ ____ ____ ____

3. I have three sides and three corners.
   What am I?

   ____ ____ ____ ____ ____ ____

4. I have four sides. Two of my sides are longer than my other two sides. What am I?

   ____ ____ ____ ____ ____

HINT Compare shapes by asking "How are they different?" and "How are they the same?"

Colour to Complete

Marlin and Dory meet many fish on their search for Nemo.

Use the Colour Key to colour the fish.

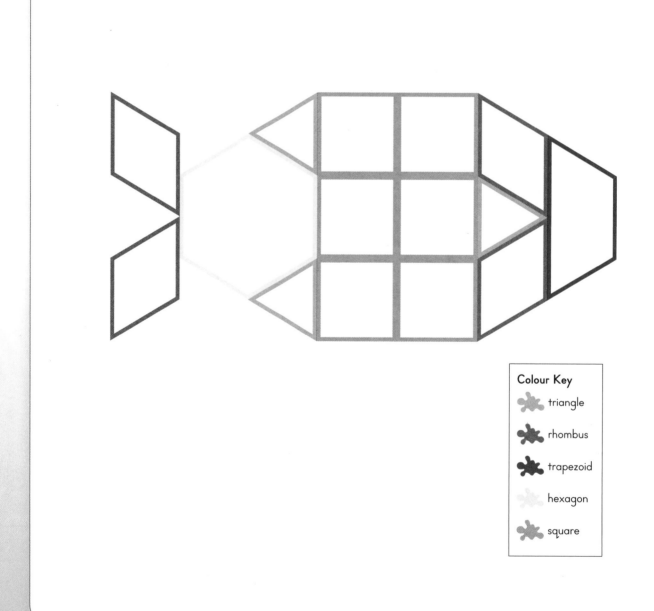

Colour Key

- triangle
- rhombus
- trapezoid
- hexagon
- square

What do Dr. Sherman and his pal use to travel on the ocean?

To find out, colour the picture. Use the Colour Key.

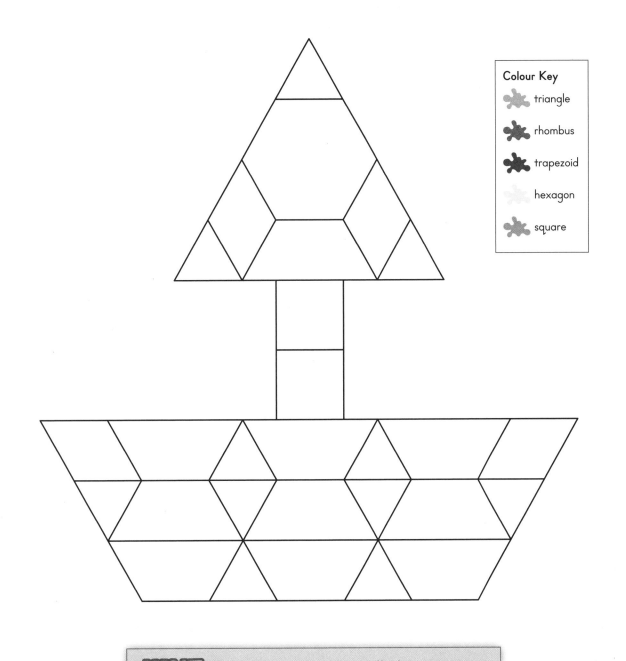

Colour Key
- triangle
- rhombus
- trapezoid
- hexagon
- square

HINT Start by colouring all the squares.
Remember that a triangle has three sides.

Colour to Complete

Prince Eric lives in a castle.

Draw a castle that uses different shapes. Label the shapes in your drawing.

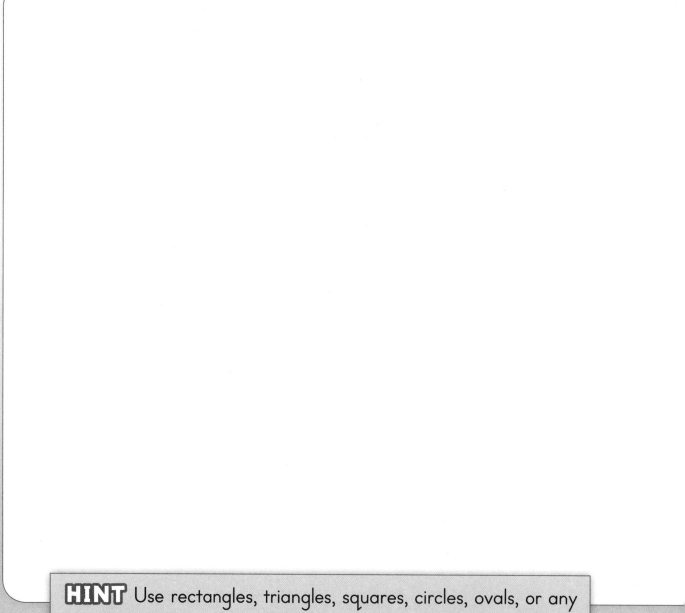

HINT Use rectangles, triangles, squares, circles, ovals, or any other 2-D shape. Use shapes of different sizes and colours.

Now draw another picture using shapes. Label the shapes in your drawing.

Matching

The Tank Gang welcomes Nemo to the aquarium. The aquarium is a **rectangular prism**. You can find **rectangles** on the sides of a rectangular prism.

Match each 3-D object to the 2-D shape you see on it. The first one is done for you.

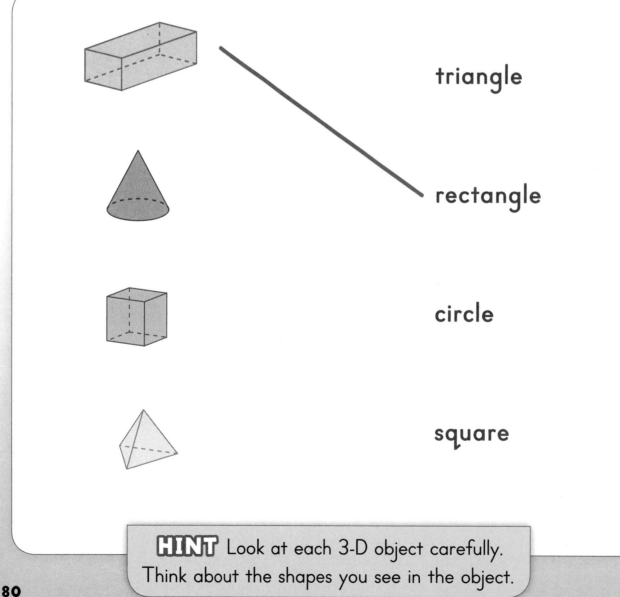

triangle

rectangle

circle

square

HINT Look at each 3-D object carefully. Think about the shapes you see in the object.

Matching

The crabs walk on pipes along the ocean floor. The pipes are shaped like cylinders.

Draw a line to match the everyday object to the 3-D object it looks like.

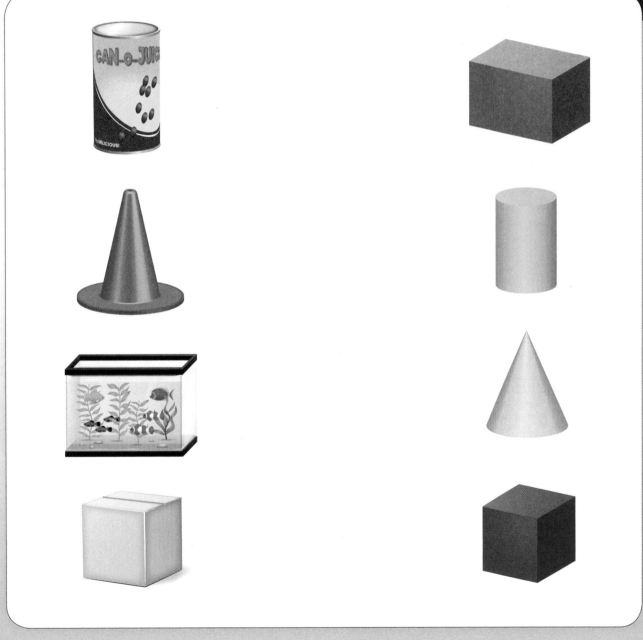

Solve the Riddles

Ursula plans to use Ariel to gain control of the undersea kingdom. She uses a magic bubble to watch Ariel and Flounder. The bubble is shaped like a sphere.

What 3-D object is most similar to each everyday object?

1. A soccer ball is shaped like a

___ ___ ___ ___ ___ ___.

Word Bank

cone

cube

cylinder

sphere

2. On a hot day, you can put ice cream in a

___ ___ ___ ___.

3. A trash bin with no handles reminds me of a

___ ___ ___ ___ ___ ___ ___.

4. A game board die is shaped like a

___ ___ ___ ___.

What everyday object is being described?

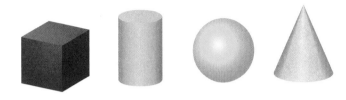

Word Bank

block   Earth   paint can   party hat

1. I look like a cylinder. I hold paint. What am I?

   —— —— —— —— ——   —— —— ——

2. I look like a cone. You wear me on your head at a party. What am I?

   —— —— —— —— ——   —— —— ——

3. I am a cube. You can play with me to stack and build.

   What am I? —— —— —— —— ——

4. I look like a sphere. I am a planet. You live on me.

   What am I? —— —— —— ——

Matching

Bubbles finds a large bubble! The shape of this bubble is symmetrical.

Create a symmetrical shape. Connect each picture on the left with a picture on the right.

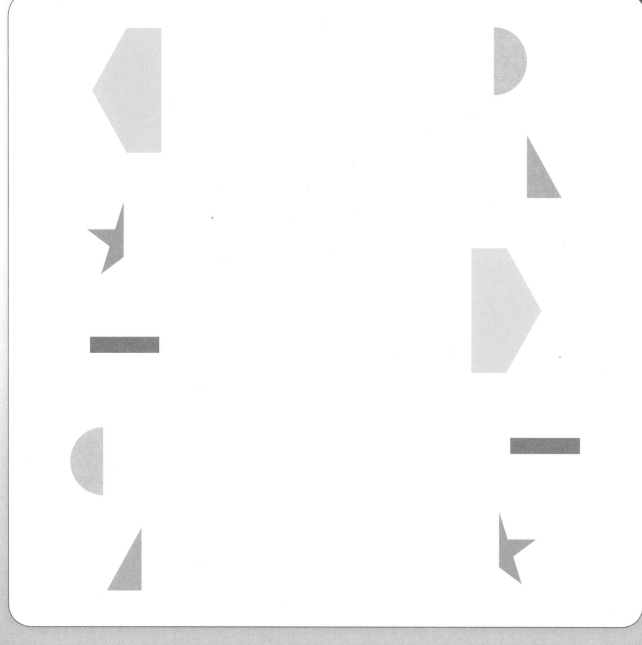

Colour to Complete

Squirt and his friend enjoy sliding on their shells.

Use the Colour Key to colour the shell. Then draw a line to show symmetry.

Colour Key
1
2
3

Word Search

Ariel is **between** her father and Eric. Prince Eric is **in front** of Ariel. King Triton is **behind** Ariel.

Circle the position words in the word search.

```
G  P  B  E  T  W  E  E  N  Q
F  V  U  R  B  B  H  I  K  K
W  B  E  L  O  W  O  R  D  X
Z  N  B  A  K  E  C  V  E  P
E  U  N  D  E  R  P  A  Y  M
L  L  A  U  Y  X  O  V  E  R
Z  Y  I  N  S  I  D  E  Z  N
B  E  S  I  D  E  F  R  W  V
N  A  B  O  V  E  K  T  P  L
M  O  U  T  S  I  D  E  U  B
```

OVER   UNDER   ABOVE   BELOW

INSIDE   OUTSIDE   BESIDE   BETWEEN

Fill In the Blanks

The statue is **between** Ariel and her father, King Triton.

Look at the image. Fill in each blank with the correct position word.

Word Bank

behind   on   in   under   inside

1. King Triton has a crown ___ ___ his head.

2. Ariel is hiding ___ ___ ___ ___ ___ the statue.

3. Ariel's collection is ___ ___ ___ ___ ___ the grotto.

4. The treasure chest is ___ ___ ___ ___ ___ the statue's arm.

5. The trident is ___ ___ King Triton's hand.

Picture Search

Nemo and his friends are back together.

Bruce is **between** his shark friends. Write the letter **B** on Bruce.

Chum has a hook **in** his nose. Write the letter **C** on Chum.

Mr. Ray swims **below** his many students. Write the letter **R** on Mr. Ray.

Dory is swimming **above** the coral. Write the letter **D** on Dory.

Nemo is **beside** his dad, Marlin. Write the letter **N** on Nemo.

Picture Search

Ariel and a group of animal friends head
for the ship. Sort the animals. Draw a
(circle) around the animals with wings.
Draw a [box] around the animals that swim.

Colour to Complete

Ariel likes to look for shells. Sort these shells by colour. (Circle) the yellow shells. Underline the purple shells.

Colour the shells to represent the number of yellow and purple shells above.

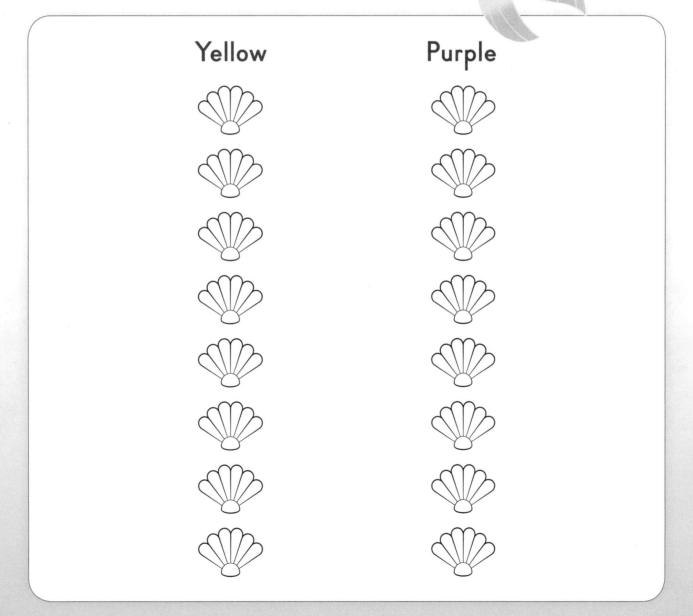

Yellow   Purple

Picture Search

Nigel is trying to help Marlin and Dory escape the seagulls. How many yellow-billed seagulls want to eat the fish? Draw tally marks to count the seagulls. Then write the number.

Tally marks:

There are _____ seagulls in the picture.

Fill In the Blanks

Gill asks Nemo to be part of his new plan. It is **likely** that Gill wants to escape from the aquarium.

Fill in the blanks to make each statement true. Use the words in the Word Bank.

Word Bank

unlikely   more likely   certain   impossible

It is ___ ___ ___ ___ ___ ___ ___ ___ for fish to learn ballet.

It is ___ ___ ___ ___ ___ ___ that fish will swim.

It is ___ ___ ___ ___ ___ ___ that fish will fly.

It is ___ ___ ___ ___ ___ ___ ___ ___ that fish will swim with other fish.

Graphing

Ariel is having her first meal with Prince Eric. There are different fruits on the table.

We asked people to pick their favourite fruit. This graph shows their response. Write a title for the graph.

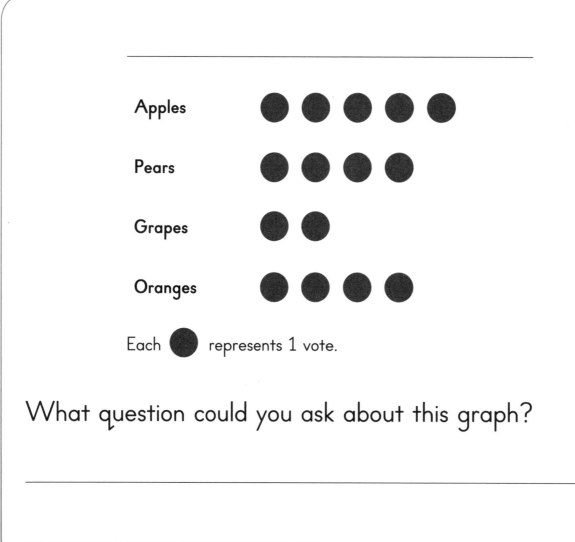

Apples

Pears

Grapes

Oranges

Each   represents 1 vote.

What question could you ask about this graph?

Ariel's best friend is Flounder. Flounder is a fish.

We asked people to pick their favourite animal. This graph shows their response. Write a title for the graph.

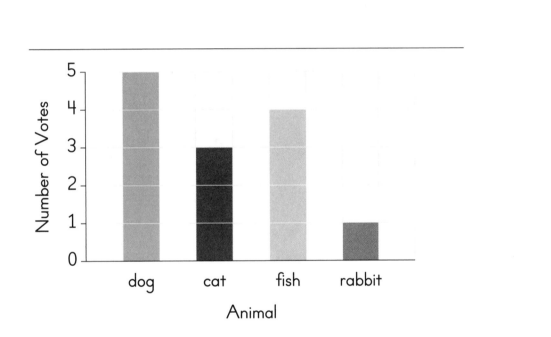

What is another question we could ask these people about animals?

_____

_____

Graphing

Lots of colourful fish live near Nemo's home.

Draw tally marks to count the fish in each group.

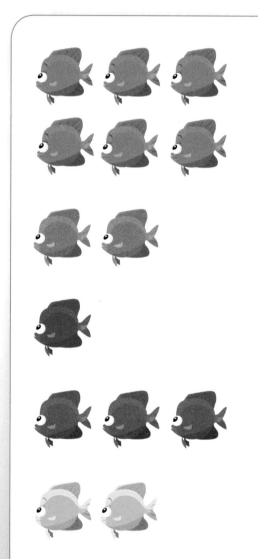

Colour	Tally

Now use the tally marks to create a pictograph. The first one is done for you.

Colours of Fish

Orange ● ● ● ● ● ●

Green

Red

Purple

Yellow

Each ● represents 1 fish.

Graphing

What do you think Ariel's favourite colour is? What about Eric's?

Sometimes it is important to find out what people like. To find out, you can take a **survey**.

Ask several people, "Look at these colours. Which colour is your favourite?" Record the votes using tally marks.

Colour	Tally
■ blue	
■ green	
■ pink	
■ purple	
■ red	

Create a bar graph to show the results of your survey.

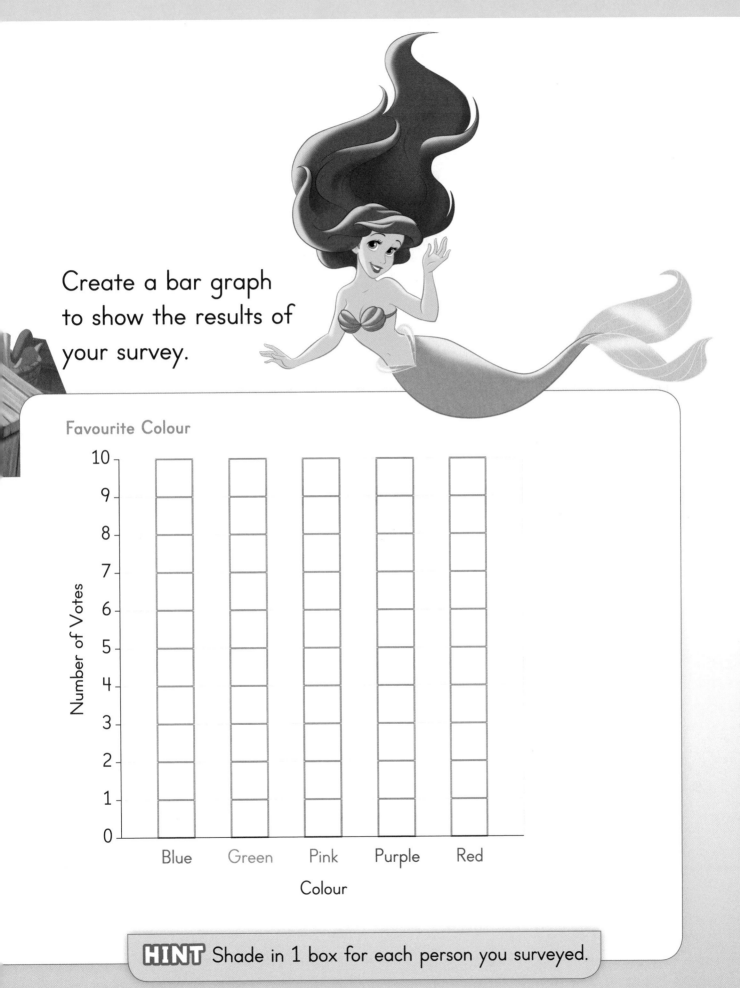

Favourite Colour

Number of Votes

10
9
8
7
6
5
4
3
2
1
0

Blue   Green   Pink   Purple   Red

Colour

HINT Shade in 1 box for each person you surveyed.

Answers

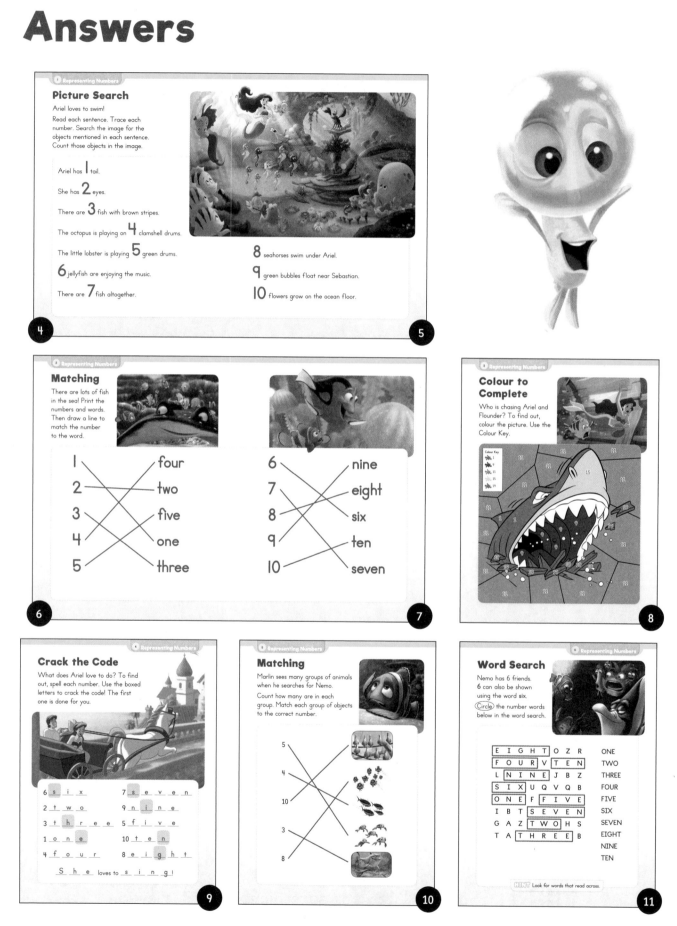

Picture Search

Ariel loves to swim!
Read each sentence. Trace each number. Search the image for the objects mentioned in each sentence. Count those objects in the image.

Ariel has **1** tail.

She has **2** eyes.

There are **3** fish with brown stripes.

The octopus is playing on **4** clamshell drums.

The little lobster is playing **5** green drums.

6 jellyfish are enjoying the music.

There are **7** fish altogether.

8 seahorses swim under Ariel.

9 green bubbles float near Sebastian.

10 flowers grow on the ocean floor.

4 5

Matching

There are lots of fish in the sea! Print the numbers and words. Then draw a line to match the number to the word.

1 — four
2 — two
3 — five
4 — one
5 — three

6 — nine
7 — eight
8 — six
9 — ten
10 — seven

6 7

Colour to Complete

Who is chasing Ariel and Flounder? To find out, colour the picture. Use the Colour Key.

Colour Key

8

Crack the Code

What does Ariel love to do? To find out, spell each number. Use the boxed letters to crack the code! The first one is done for you.

6 s i x   7 s e v e n
2 t w o   9 n i n e
3 t h r e e 5 f i v e
1 o n e   10 t e n
4 f o u r   8 e i g h t

S h e loves to s i n g!

9

Matching

Marlin sees many groups of animals when he searches for Nemo.
Count how many are in each group. Match each group of objects to the correct number.

5
4
10
3
8

10

Word Search

Nemo has 6 friends. 6 can also be shown using the word six. Circle the number words below in the word search.

E	I	G	H	T	O	Z	R
F	O	U	R	V	T	E	N
L	N	I	N	E	J	B	Z
S	I	X	U	Q	V	Q	B
O	N	E	F	F	I	V	E
I	B	T	S	E	V	E	N
G	A	Z	T	W	O	H	S
T	A	T	H	R	E	E	B

ONE
TWO
THREE
FOUR
FIVE
SIX
SEVEN
EIGHT
NINE
TEN

HINT Look for words that read across.

11

100

*Sample answers provided.

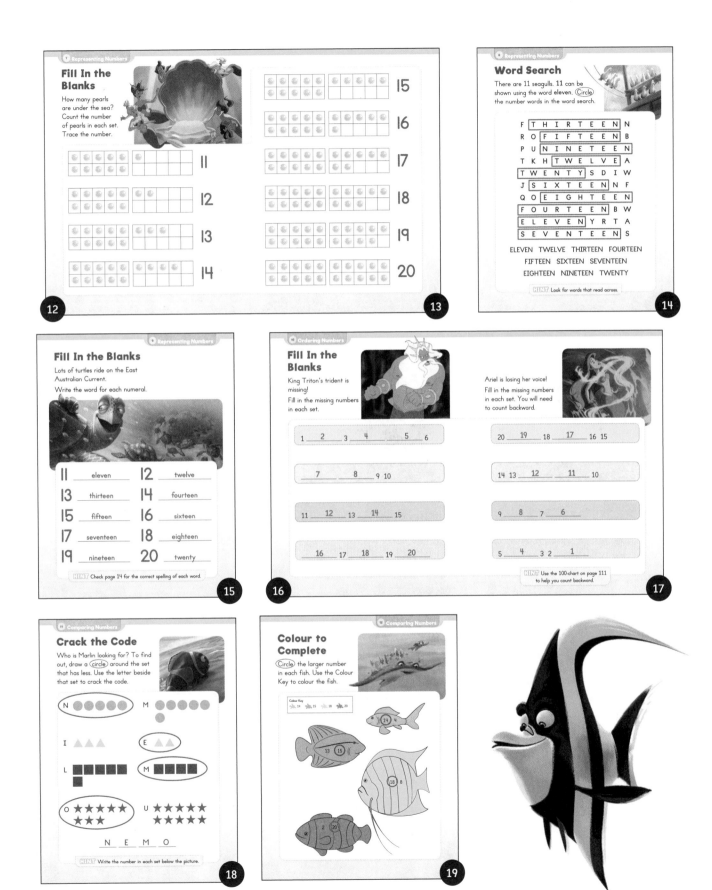

Fill In the Blanks

How many pearls are under the sea? Count the number of pearls in each set. Trace the number.

11
12
13
14
15
16
17
18
19
20

Word Search

There are 11 seagulls. 11 can be shown using the word **eleven**. Circle the number words in the word search.

```
F T H I R T E E N N
R O F I F T E E N B
P U N I N E T E E N
T K H T W E L V E A
T W E N T Y S D I W
J S I X T E E N N F
Q O E I G H T E E N
F O U R T E E N B W
E L E V E N Y R T A
S E V E N T E E N S
```

ELEVEN TWELVE THIRTEEN FOURTEEN
FIFTEEN SIXTEEN SEVENTEEN
EIGHTEEN NINETEEN TWENTY

HINT Look for words that read across.

Fill In the Blanks

Lots of turtles ride on the East Australian Current.

Write the word for each numeral.

11 eleven
12 twelve
13 thirteen
14 fourteen
15 fifteen
16 sixteen
17 seventeen
18 eighteen
19 nineteen
20 twenty

HINT Check page 14 for the correct spelling of each word.

Fill In the Blanks

King Triton's trident is missing! Fill in the missing numbers in each set.

Ariel is losing her voice! Fill in the missing numbers in each set. You will need to count backward.

1 _2_ 3 _4_ _5_ 6
_7_ _8_ 9 10
11 _12_ 13 _14_ 15
16 17 _18_ 19 _20_

20 _19_ 18 _17_ 16 15
14 13 _12_ _11_ 10
9 _8_ 7 _6_
5 _4_ 3 2 _1_

HINT Use the 100-chart on page 111 to help you count backward.

Crack the Code

Who is Marlin looking for? To find out, draw a circle around the set that has less. Use the letter beside that set to crack the code.

N ●●●●●
M ●●●● ●

I ▲▲▲
E ▲▲

L ■■■■ ■
M ■■■

O ★★★★★ ★★★
U ★★★★★ ★★★★★

N E M O

HINT Write the number in each set below the picture.

Colour to Complete

Circle the larger number in each fish. Use the Colour Key to colour the fish.

Colour Key
14   15   18   20

14 4
13 15
18 8
2 20

*Sample answers provided.

Answers

Picture Search

Try to estimate how many friends have gathered to welcome Nemo back! How many animals are in each picture?

I estimate there are about __*15__ animals.

I estimate there are about __*5__ animals.

I estimate there are about __*12__ animals.

I estimate there are about __*12__ animals.

I estimate there are about __*9__ fish eyes.

20   21

Fill In the Blanks

Many animals live in the sea. Estimate how many animals are in each set. Then count them to check your estimate.

I estimate there are about __*5__ dolphins.

There are __6__ dolphins.

I estimate there are about __*17__ seahorses.

There are __15__ seahorses.

I estimate there are about __*10__ fish.

There are __9__ fish.

HINT It is great when your estimate is close to the actual number, but it is all right for your estimate to not be the actual number!

22

Picture Search

Prince Eric likes to sail the ocean and see lots of creatures!

Estimate how many squid are in this array. Then count them to check your estimate.

I estimate there are about __*25__ squid.

There are __30__ squid.

Was your estimate close to the number you counted?

__*Yes__

HINT Look at the number of squid in each group to help you guess more accurately.

23

Fill In the Blanks

How many merpeople are swimming in the sea? Estimate how many. Then count.

I estimate that there are about __*4__ merpeople swimming in the sea.

I count __2__ merpeople swimming in the sea.

Look at the image again. Now estimate how many fish there are.

I estimate that there are about __*10__ fish swimming in the sea.

I count __12__ fish swimming in the sea.

How many shells are in each set? Estimate the number. Then count.

I estimate that there are about __*10__ peach shells.

I count __12__ peach shells.

I estimate that there are about __*15__ pink shells.

I count __18__ pink shells.

I estimate that there are about __*18__ purple shells.

I count __20__ purple shells.

24   25

Matching

Bubbles waits beside the treasure chest. How much money might the chest hold? Draw a line to match each coin to its correct value.

- 10¢
- 25¢
- $1
- 5¢
- $2

26

Maze

Dr. Sherman spends money to care for his fish. Start with the coin with the lowest value. Make your way to the coin with the highest value.

Start

Finish

27

Picture Search

Ariel and her friends are lining up to dance. Ariel is first in line. Draw a box around the second friend in line. Circle the third friend in the line. Underline the fourth friend in line.

28

102

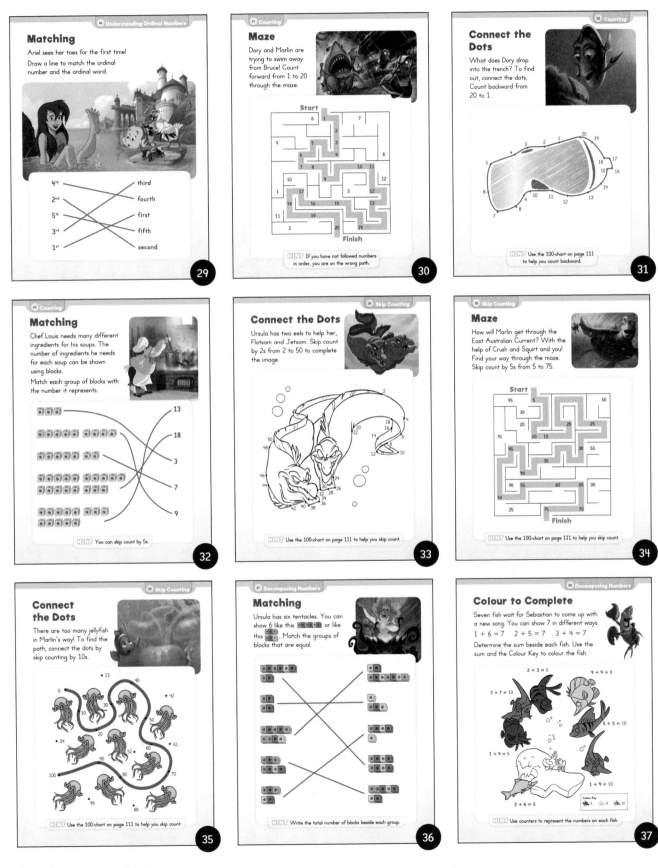

Matching

Ariel sees her toes for the first time!
Draw a line to match the ordinal
number and the ordinal word.

4ᵗʰ   third
2ⁿᵈ   fourth
5ᵗʰ   first
3ʳᵈ   fifth
1ˢᵗ   second

29

Maze

Dory and Marlin are
trying to swim away
from Bruce! Count
forward from 1 to 20
through the maze.

Start

Finish

HINT If you have not followed numbers
in order, you are on the wrong path.

30

Connect the Dots

What does Dory drop
into the trench? To find
out, connect the dots.
Count backward from
20 to 1.

HINT Use the 100-chart on page 111
to help you count backward.

31

Matching

Chef Louis needs many different
ingredients for his soups. The
number of ingredients he needs
for each soup can be shown
using blocks.

Match each group of blocks with
the number it represents.

13
18
3
7
9

HINT You can skip count by 5s.

32

Connect the Dots

Ursula has two eels to help her,
Flotsam and Jetsam. Skip count
by 2s from 2 to 50 to complete
the image.

HINT Use the 100-chart on page 111 to help you skip count.

33

Maze

How will Marlin get through the
East Australian Current? With the
help of Crush and Squirt and you!
Find your way through the maze.
Skip count by 5s from 5 to 75.

Start

Finish

HINT Use the 100-chart on page 111 to help you skip count.

34

Connect the Dots

There are too many jellyfish
in Marlin's way! To find the
path, connect the dots by
skip counting by 10s.

HINT Use the 100-chart on page 111 to help you skip count.

35

Matching

Ursula has six tentacles. You can
show 6 like this or like
this. Match the groups of
blocks that are equal.

HINT Write the total number of blocks beside each group.

36

Colour to Complete

Seven fish wait for Sebastian to come up with
a new song. You can show 7 in different ways.
$1 + 6 = 7$ $2 + 5 = 7$ $3 + 4 = 7$
Determine the sum beside each fish. Use the
sum and the Colour Key to colour the fish.

$2 + 3 = 5$ $4 + 4 = 8$
$3 + 7 = 10$
                    $5 + 5 = 10$
$1 + 4 = 5$
                    $1 + 9 = 10$
$2 + 6 = 8$
        Colour Key
        5   8   10

HINT Use counters to represent the numbers on each fish.

37

*Sample answers provided.

Answers

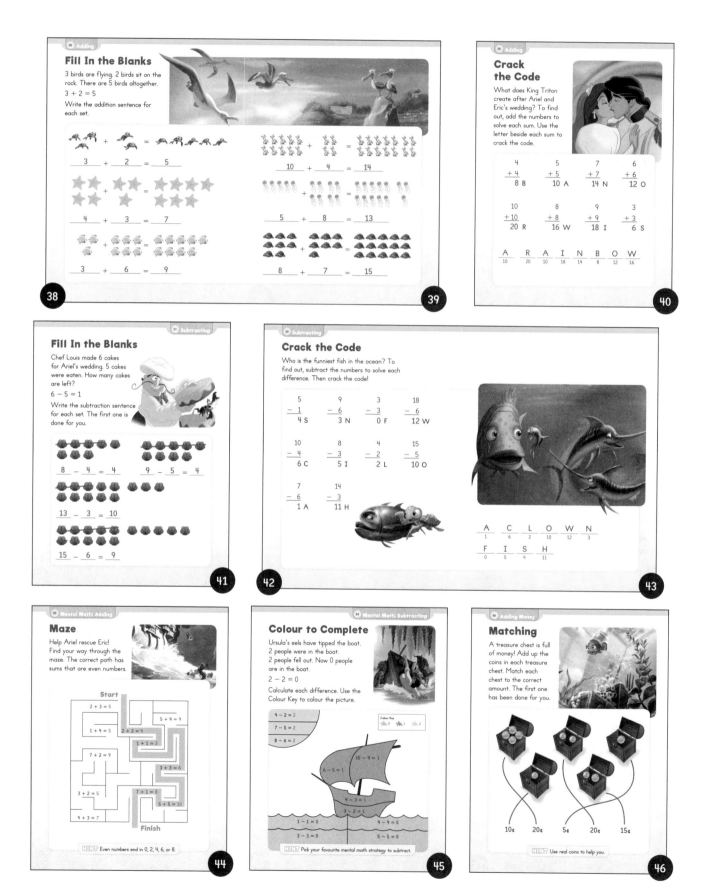

Fill In the Blanks

3 birds are flying. 2 birds sit on the rock. There are 5 birds altogether.

3 + 2 = 5

Write the addition sentence for each set.

3 + 2 = 5

10 + 4 = 14

4 + 3 = 7

5 + 8 = 13

3 + 6 = 9

8 + 7 = 15

38

39

Crack the Code

What does King Triton create after Ariel and Eric's wedding? To find out, add the numbers to solve each sum. Use the letter beside each sum to crack the code.

4	5	7	6
+ 4	+ 5	+ 7	+ 6
8 B	10 A	14 N	12 O

10	8	9	3
+ 10	+ 8	+ 9	+ 3
20 R	16 W	18 I	6 S

A R A I N B O W
10 20 10 18 14 8 12 16

40

Fill In the Blanks

Chef Louis made 6 cakes for Ariel's wedding. 5 cakes were eaten. How many cakes are left?

6 − 5 = 1

Write the subtraction sentence for each set. The first one is done for you.

8 − 4 = 4

9 − 5 = 4

13 − 3 = 10

15 − 6 = 9

41

Crack the Code

Who is the funniest fish in the ocean? To find out, subtract the numbers to solve each difference. Then crack the code!

5	9	3	18
− 1	− 6	− 3	− 6
4 S	3 N	0 F	12 W

10	8	4	15
− 4	− 3	− 2	− 5
6 C	5 I	2 L	10 O

7	14
− 6	− 3
1 A	11 H

A C L O W N
1 6 2 10 12 3

F I S H
0 5 4 11

42

43

Maze

Help Ariel rescue Eric! Find your way through the maze. The correct path has sums that are even numbers.

Start

2 + 3 = 5

5 + 4 = 9

1 + 4 = 5   2 + 2 = 4

1 + 1 = 2

7 + 2 = 9

3 + 3 = 6

3 + 2 = 5   7 + 1 = 8

5 + 5 = 10

4 + 3 = 7

Finish

HINT Even numbers end in 0, 2, 4, 6, or 8.

44

Colour to Complete

Ursula's eels have tipped the boat. 2 people were in the boat. 2 people fell out. Now 0 people are in the boat.

2 − 2 = 0

Calculate each difference. Use the Colour Key to colour the picture.

4 − 2 = 2

7 − 5 = 2

8 − 6 = 2

Colour Key
0   1   2

10 − 9 = 1

6 − 5 = 1

4 − 3 = 1

3 − 2 = 1

1 − 0 = 0

4 − 4 = 0

3 − 3 = 0

5 − 5 = 0

HINT Pick your favourite mental math strategy to subtract.

45

Matching

A treasure chest is full of money! Add up the coins in each treasure chest. Match each chest to the correct amount. The first one is done for you.

10¢   20¢   5¢   20¢   15¢

HINT Use real coins to help you.

46

104

*Sample answers provided.

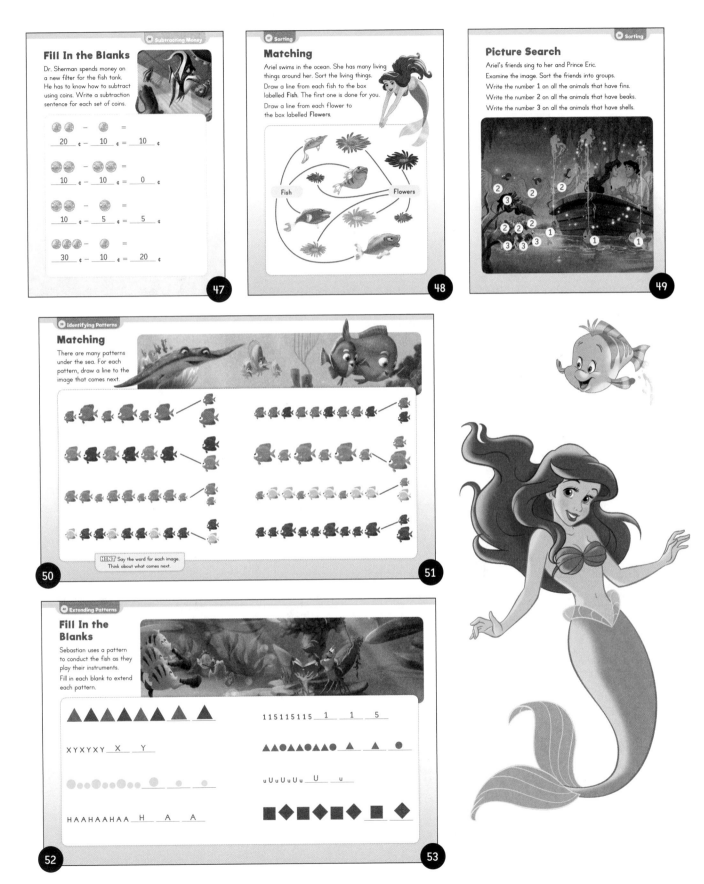

Fill In the Blanks

Dr. Sherman spends money on a new filter for the fish tank. He has to know how to subtract using coins. Write a subtraction sentence for each set of coins.

20 ¢ − 10 ¢ = 10 ¢

10 ¢ − 10 ¢ = 0 ¢

10 ¢ − 5 ¢ = 5 ¢

30 ¢ − 10 ¢ = 20 ¢

47

Matching

Ariel swims in the ocean. She has many living things around her. Sort the living things.

Draw a line from each fish to the box labelled **Fish**. The first one is done for you.

Draw a line from each flower to the box labelled **Flowers**.

Fish   Flowers

48

Picture Search

Ariel's friends sing to her and Prince Eric. Examine the image. Sort the friends into groups.
Write the number **1** on all the animals that have fins.
Write the number **2** on all the animals that have beaks.
Write the number **3** on all the animals that have shells.

49

Matching

There are many patterns under the sea. For each pattern, draw a line to the image that comes next.

HINT Say the word for each image. Think about what comes next.

50   51

Fill In the Blanks

Sebastian uses a pattern to conduct the fish as they play their instruments. Fill in each blank to extend each pattern.

▲▲▲▲▲▲ ▲ ▲ ▲

X Y X Y X Y X Y

● ● ● ● ● ● ● ● ● ● ●

H A A H A A H A A H A A

1 1 5 1 1 5 1 1 5 1   1   5

▲▲●▲▲●▲▲● ▲ ▲ ●

u U u U u U u U U U

■ ◆ ■ ◆ ■ ◆ ■ ◆

52   53

*Sample answers provided.

Answers

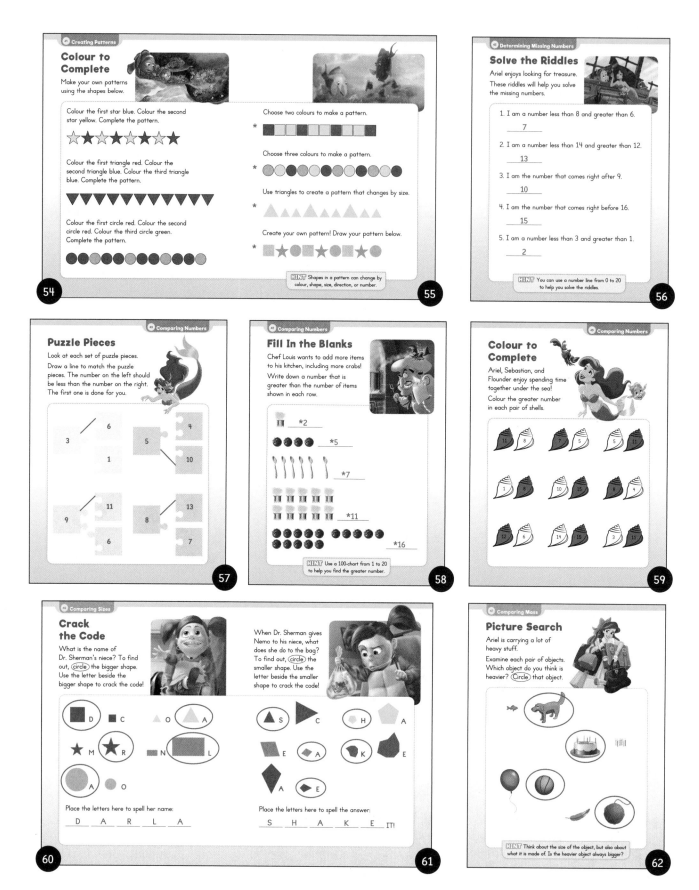

Colour to Complete
(Creating Patterns)

Make your own patterns using the shapes below.

Colour the first star blue. Colour the second star yellow. Complete the pattern.

Colour the first triangle red. Colour the second triangle blue. Colour the third triangle blue. Complete the pattern.

Colour the first circle red. Colour the second circle red. Colour the third circle green. Complete the pattern.

Choose two colours to make a pattern.

Choose three colours to make a pattern.

Use triangles to create a pattern that changes by size.

Create your own pattern! Draw your pattern below.

HINT Shapes in a pattern can change by colour, shape, size, direction, or number.

54

Solve the Riddles
(Determining Missing Numbers)

Ariel enjoys looking for treasure. These riddles will help you solve the missing numbers.

1. I am a number less than 8 and greater than 6.
   _7_
2. I am a number less than 14 and greater than 12.
   _13_
3. I am the number that comes right after 9.
   _10_
4. I am the number that comes right before 16.
   _15_
5. I am a number less than 3 and greater than 1.
   _2_

HINT You can use a number line from 0 to 20 to help you solve the riddles.

55   **56**

Puzzle Pieces
(Comparing Numbers)

Look at each set of puzzle pieces. Draw a line to match the puzzle pieces. The number on the left should be less than the number on the right. The first one is done for you.

3 — 6
1
5 — 10
4

9 — 11
6
8 — 13
7

57

Fill In the Blanks
(Comparing Numbers)

Chef Louis wants to add more items to his kitchen, including more crabs! Write down a number that is greater than the number of items shown in each row.

*2
*5
*7
*11
*16

HINT Use a 100-chart from 1 to 20 to help you find the greater number.

58

Colour to Complete
(Comparing Numbers)

Ariel, Sebastian, and Flounder enjoy spending time together under the sea!
Colour the greater number in each pair of shells.

11 8   7 5   5 11
1 8   10 15   8 4
12 6   14 15   3 11

59

Crack the Code
(Comparing Sizes)

What is the name of Dr. Sherman's niece? To find out, circle the bigger shape. Use the letter beside the bigger shape to crack the code!

D C   O A
M R   N L
A O

Place the letters here to spell her name:
D A R L A

When Dr. Sherman gives Nemo to his niece, what does she do to the bag? To find out, circle the smaller shape. Use the letter beside the smaller shape to crack the code!

S C   H A
E A   K E
A E

Place the letters here to spell the answer:
S H A K E IT!

60   **61**

Picture Search
(Comparing Mass)

Ariel is carrying a lot of heavy stuff.
Examine each pair of objects. Which object do you think is heavier? Circle that object.

HINT Think about the size of the object, but also about what it is made of. Is the heavier object always bigger?

62

106

*Sample answers provided.

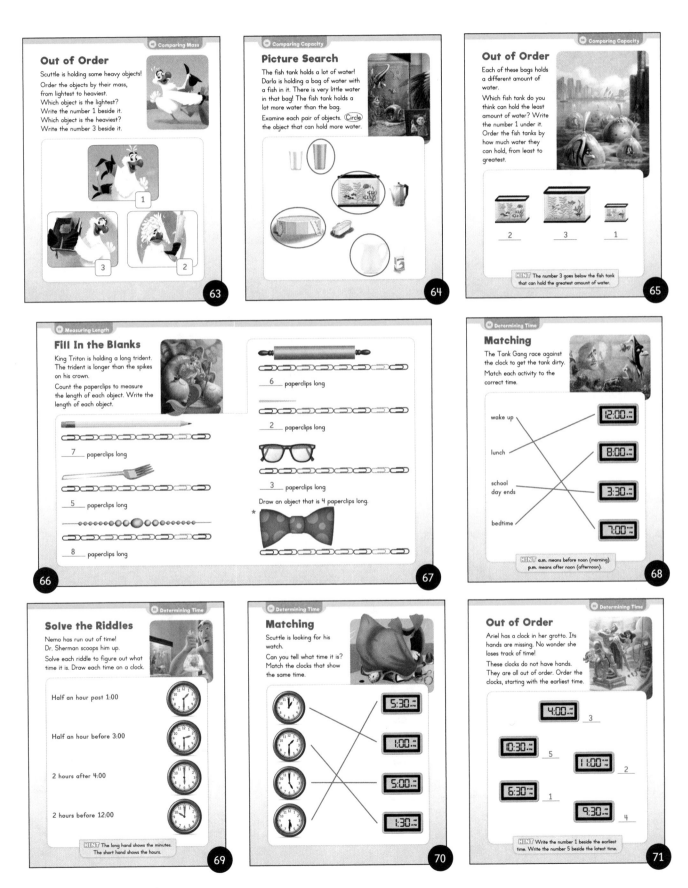

Out of Order

Scuttle is holding some heavy objects!

Order the objects by their mass, from lightest to heaviest.
Which object is the lightest? Write the number 1 beside it.
Which object is the heaviest? Write the number 3 beside it.

1

3

2

63

Picture Search

The fish tank holds a lot of water! Darla is holding a bag of water with a fish in it. There is very little water in that bag! The fish tank holds a lot more water than the bag.

Examine each pair of objects. Circle the object that can hold more water.

64

Out of Order

Each of these bags holds a different amount of water.

Which fish tank do you think can hold the least amount of water? Write the number 1 under it. Order the fish tanks by how much water they can hold, from least to greatest.

2   3   1

HINT The number 3 goes below the fish tank that can hold the greatest amount of water.

65

Fill In the Blanks

King Triton is holding a long trident. The trident is longer than the spikes on his crown.

Count the paperclips to measure the length of each object. Write the length of each object.

7 paperclips long

5 paperclips long

8 paperclips long

6 paperclips long

2 paperclips long

3 paperclips long

Draw an object that is 4 paperclips long.

*

66

67

Matching

The Tank Gang race against the clock to get the tank dirty.

Match each activity to the correct time.

wake up

lunch

school day ends

bedtime

12:00
8:00
3:30
7:00

HINT a.m. means before noon (morning). p.m. means after noon (afternoon).

68

Solve the Riddles

Nemo has run out of time! Dr. Sherman scoops him up.

Solve each riddle to figure out what time it is. Draw each time on a clock.

Half an hour past 1:00

Half an hour before 3:00

2 hours after 4:00

2 hours before 12:00

HINT The long hand shows the minutes. The short hand shows the hours.

69

Matching

Scuttle is looking for his watch.

Can you tell what time it is? Match the clocks that show the same time.

5:30
1:00
5:00
1:30

70

Out of Order

Ariel has a clock in her grotto. Its hands are missing. No wonder she loses track of time!

These clocks do not have hands. They are all out of order. Order the clocks, starting with the earliest time.

4:00   3

10:30   5

11:00   2

6:30   1

9:30   4

HINT Write the number 1 beside the earliest time. Write the number 5 beside the latest time.

71

Answers

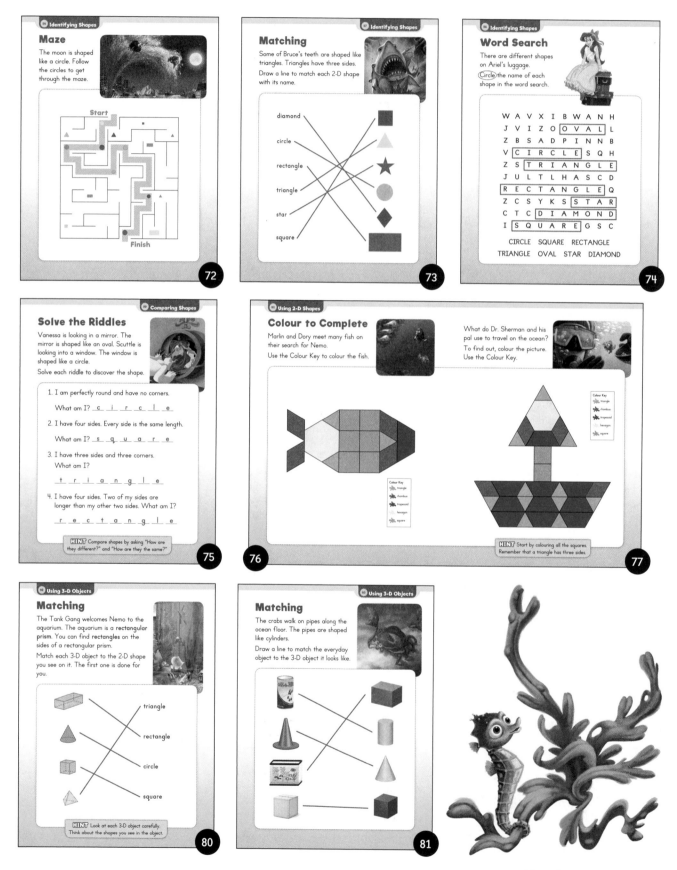

Maze

The moon is shaped like a circle. Follow the circles to get through the maze.

Identifying Shapes

Start

Finish

72

Matching

Some of Bruce's teeth are shaped like triangles. Triangles have three sides.
Draw a line to match each 2-D shape with its name.

Identifying Shapes

diamond
circle
rectangle
triangle
star
square

73

Word Search

There are different shapes on Ariel's luggage.
Circle the name of each shape in the word search.

Identifying Shapes

```
W A V X I B W A N H
J V I Z O O V A L L
Z B S A D P I N N B
V C I R C L E S Q H
Z S T R I A N G L E
J U L T H A S C D
R E C T A N G L E Q
Z C S Y K S S T A R
C T C D I A M O N D
I S Q U A R E G S C
```

CIRCLE   SQUARE   RECTANGLE
TRIANGLE   OVAL   STAR   DIAMOND

74

Solve the Riddles

Vanessa is looking in a mirror. The mirror is shaped like an oval. Scuttle is looking into a window. The window is shaped like a circle.
Solve each riddle to discover the shape.

Comparing Shapes

1. I am perfectly round and have no corners.
   What am I? c i r c l e

2. I have four sides. Every side is the same length.
   What am I? s q u a r e

3. I have three sides and three corners.
   What am I?
   t r i a n g l e

4. I have four sides. Two of my sides are longer than my other two sides. What am I?
   r e c t a n g l e

HINT Compare shapes by asking "How are they different?" and "How are they the same?"

75

Colour to Complete

Marlin and Dory meet many fish on their search for Nemo.
Use the Colour Key to colour the fish.

Using 2-D Shapes

What do Dr. Sherman and his pal use to travel on the ocean? To find out, colour the picture. Use the Colour Key.

Colour Key
triangle
rhombus
trapezoid
hexagon
square

Colour Key
triangle
rhombus
trapezoid
hexagon
square

HINT Start by colouring all the squares. Remember that a triangle has three sides.

76   **77**

Matching

The Tank Gang welcomes Nemo to the aquarium. The aquarium is a **rectangular prism**. You can find **rectangles** on the sides of a rectangular prism.
Match each 3-D object to the 2-D shape you see on it. The first one is done for you.

Using 3-D Objects

triangle
rectangle
circle
square

HINT Look at each 3-D object carefully. Think about the shapes you see in the object.

80

Matching

The crabs walk on pipes along the ocean floor. The pipes are shaped like cylinders.
Draw a line to match the everyday object to the 3-D object it looks like.

Using 3-D Objects

81

108

*Sample answers provided.

Page 82 — Using 3-D Objects

Solve the Riddles

Ursula plans to use Ariel to gain control of the undersea kingdom. She uses a magic bubble to watch Ariel and Flounder. The bubble is shaped like a sphere. What 3-D object is most similar to each everyday object?

1. A soccer ball is shaped like a
s p h e r e

2. On a hot day, you can put ice cream in a
c o n e

3. A trash bin with no handles reminds me of a
c y l i n d e r

4. A game board die is shaped like a
c u b e

Word Bank

cone
cube
cylinder
sphere

Page 83

What everyday object is being described?

Word Bank

block Earth paint can party hat

1. I look like a cylinder. I hold paint. What am I?
p a i n t   c a n

2. I look like a cone. You wear me on your head at a party. What am I?
p a r t y   h a t

3. I am a cube. You can play with me to stack and build.
What am I? b l o c k

4. I look like a sphere. I am a planet. You live on me.
What am I? E a r t h

Page 84 — Identifying Symmetry

Matching

Bubbles finds a large bubble! The shape of this bubble is symmetrical.
Create a symmetrical shape. Connect each picture on the left with a picture on the right.

Page 85 — Identifying Symmetry

Colour to Complete

Squirt and his friend enjoy sliding on their shells.
Use the Colour Key to colour the shell. Then draw a line to show symmetry.

Colour Key
1
2
3

Page 86 — Identifying Location

Word Search

Ariel is between her father and Eric. Prince Eric is in front of Ariel. King Triton is behind Ariel. Circle the position words in the word search.

```
G P B E T W E E N Q
F V U R B B H I K K
W B E L O W O R D X
Z N B A K E C V E P
E U N D E R P A Y M
L L A U Y X O V E R
Z Y I N S I D E Z N
B E S I D E F R W V
N A B O V E K T P L
M O U T S I D E U B
```

OVER UNDER ABOVE BELOW
INSIDE OUTSIDE BESIDE BETWEEN

Page 87 — Identifying Location

Fill In the Blanks

The statue is between Ariel and her father, King Triton. Look at the image. Fill in each blank with the correct position word.

Word Bank

behind on in under inside

1. King Triton has a crown o n his head.
2. Ariel is hiding b e h i n d the statue.
3. Ariel's collection is i n s i d e the grotto.
4. The treasure chest is u n d e r the statue's arm.
5. The trident is i n King Triton's hand.

Page 88 / 89 — Identifying Location

Picture Search

Nemo and his friends are back together.

Bruce is **between** his shark friends. Write the letter B on Bruce.

Chum has a hook in his nose. Write the letter C on Chum.

Mr. Ray swims **below** his many students. Write the letter R on Mr. Ray.

Dory is swimming **above** the coral. Write the letter D on Dory.

Nemo is **beside** his dad, Marlin. Write the letter N on Nemo.

Page 90 — Collecting and Sorting Data

Picture Search

Ariel and a group of animal friends head for the ship. Sort the animals. Draw a circle around the animals with wings. Draw a box around the animals that swim.

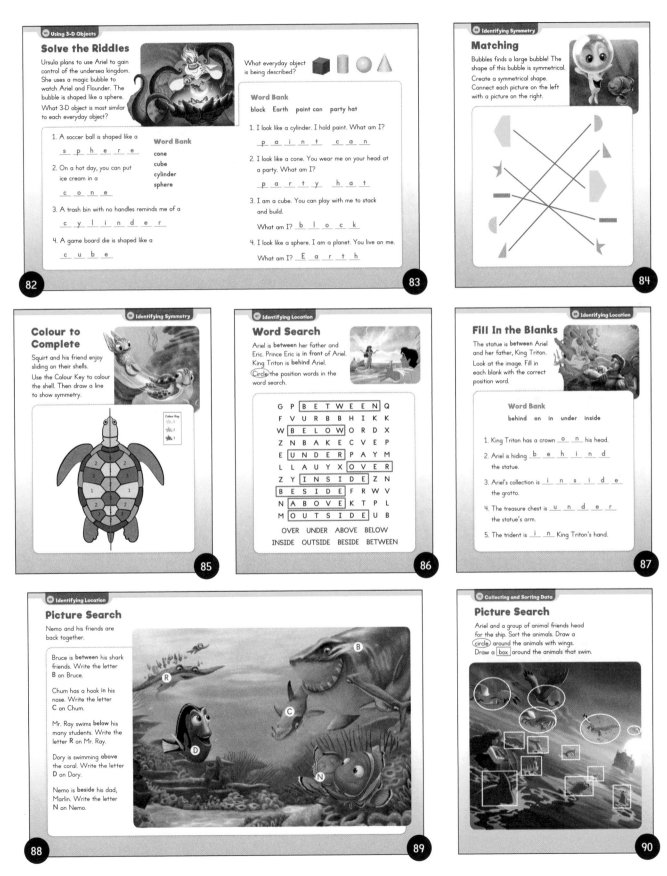

*Sample answers provided.

Answers

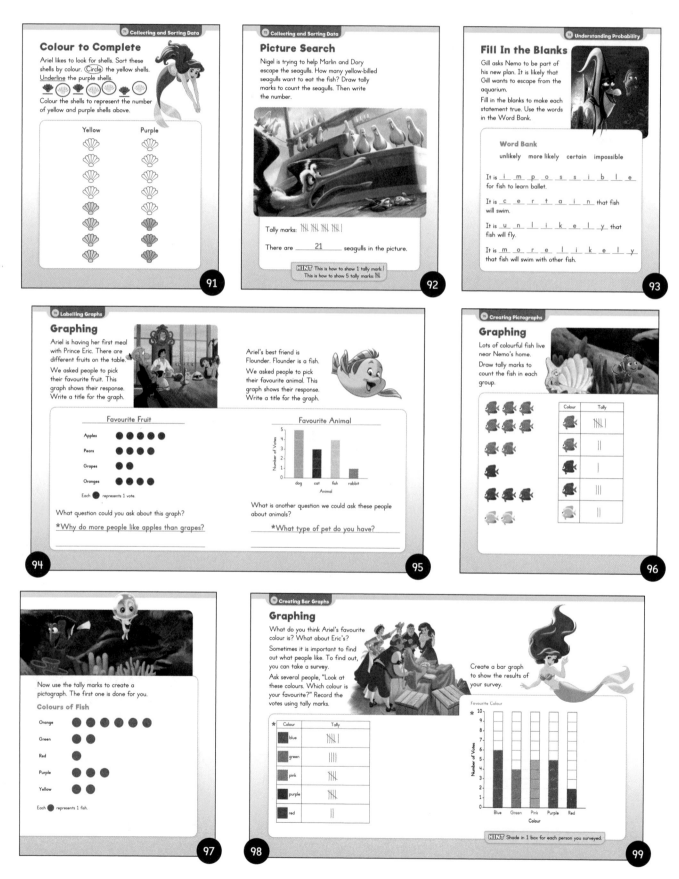

Colour to Complete — Collecting and Sorting Data
Ariel likes to look for shells. Sort these shells by colour. (Circle) the yellow shells. Underline the purple shells.
Colour the shells to represent the number of yellow and purple shells above.

Yellow | Purple

Picture Search — Collecting and Sorting Data
Nigel is trying to help Marlin and Dory escape the seagulls. How many yellow-billed seagulls want to eat the fish? Draw tally marks to count the seagulls. Then write the number.

Tally marks: ||||| ||||| ||||| ||||| |
There are ___21___ seagulls in the picture.

HINT This is how to show 1 tally mark: |
This is how to show 5 tally marks: |||||

Fill In the Blanks — Understanding Probability
Gill asks Nemo to be part of his new plan. It is likely that Gill wants to escape from the aquarium.
Fill in the blanks to make each statement true. Use the words in the Word Bank.

Word Bank
unlikely   more likely   certain   impossible

It is i m p o s s i b l e for fish to learn ballet.

It is c e r t a i n that fish will swim.

It is u n l i k e l y that fish will fly.

It is m o r e   l i k e l y that fish will swim with other fish.

91 · **92** · **93**

Graphing — Labelling Graphs
Ariel is having her first meal with Prince Eric. There are different fruits on the table.
We asked people to pick their favourite fruit. This graph shows their response. Write a title for the graph.

Favourite Fruit
Apples
Pears
Grapes
Oranges
Each ● represents 1 vote.

What question could you ask about this graph?
*Why do more people like apples than grapes?

Ariel's best friend is Flounder. Flounder is a fish. We asked people to pick their favourite animal. This graph shows their response. Write a title for the graph.

Favourite Animal

What is another question we could ask these people about animals?
*What type of pet do you have?

Graphing — Creating Pictographs
Lots of colourful fish live near Nemo's home. Draw tally marks to count the fish in each group.

Colour	Tally

94 · **95** · **96**

Now use the tally marks to create a pictograph. The first one is done for you.

Colours of Fish
Orange
Green
Red
Purple
Yellow
Each ● represents 1 fish.

Graphing — Creating Bar Graphs
What do you think Ariel's favourite colour is? What about Eric's?
Sometimes it is important to find out what people like. To find out, you can take a survey.
Ask several people, "Look at these colours. Which colour is your favourite?" Record the votes using tally marks.

*	Colour	Tally
	blue	|||||	
	green	||||
	pink	|||||
	purple	|||||
	red	||

Create a bar graph to show the results of your survey.

Favourite Colour

HINT Shade in 1 box for each person you surveyed.

97 · **98** · **99**

110

*Sample answers provided.

Learning Tools

1	2	3	4	5	6	7	8	9	10
11	12	13	14	15	16	17	18	19	20
21	22	23	24	25	26	27	28	29	30
31	32	33	34	35	36	37	38	39	40
41	42	43	44	45	46	47	48	49	50
51	52	53	54	55	56	57	58	59	60
61	62	63	64	65	66	67	68	69	70
71	72	73	74	75	76	77	78	79	80
81	82	83	84	85	86	87	88	89	90
91	92	93	94	95	96	97	98	99	100

Cut out these flash cards. Use them to practise numbers and number words.

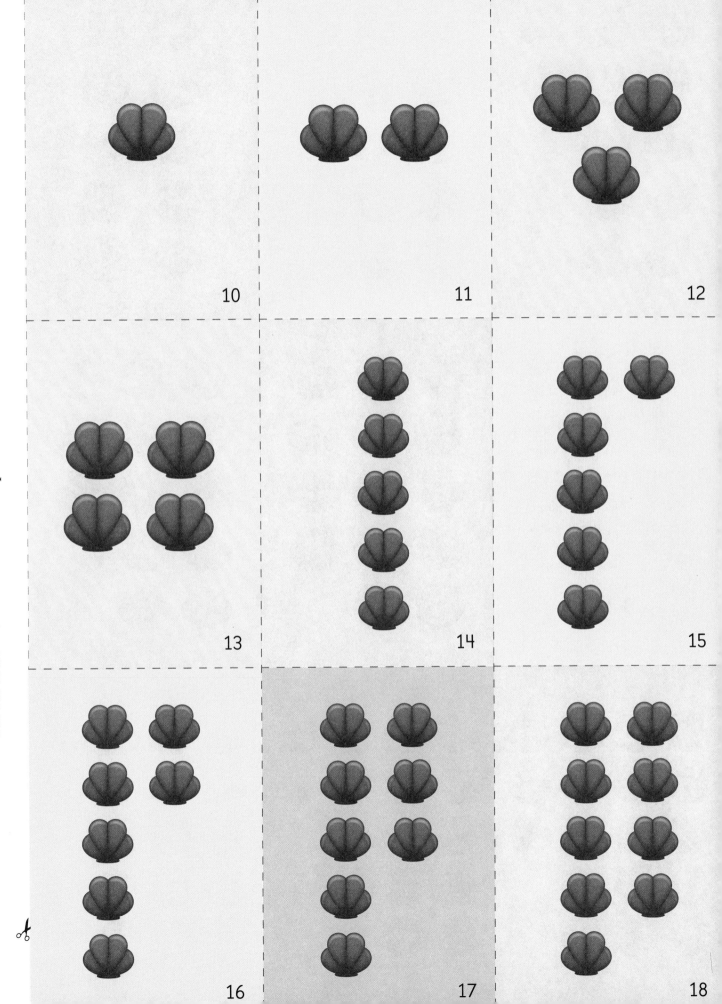

10

11

12

13

14

15

16

17

18

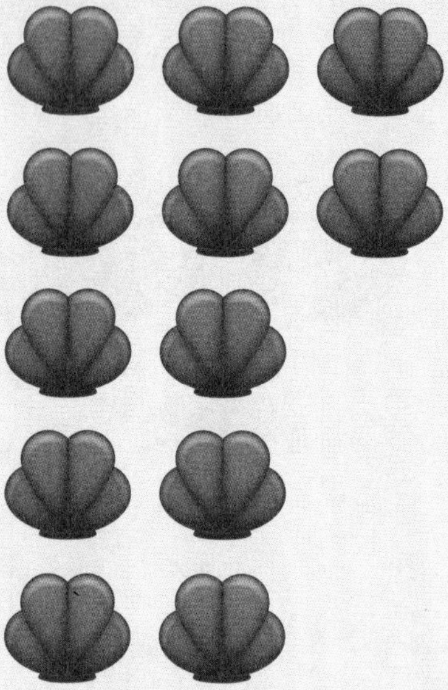

3

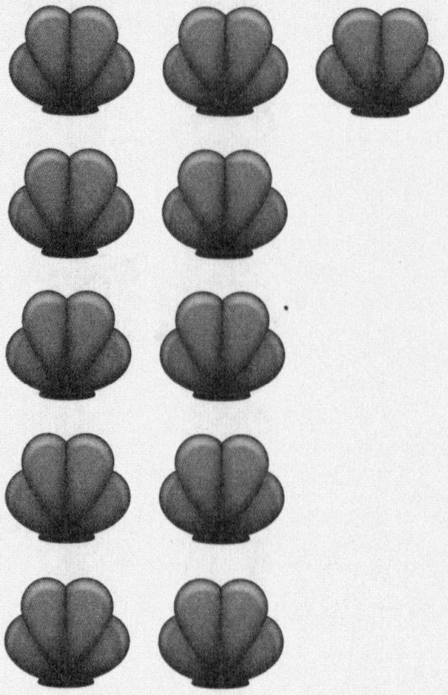

2

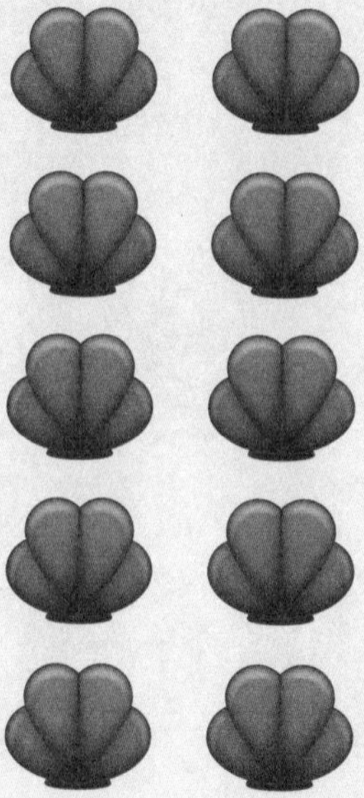

1

6

5

4

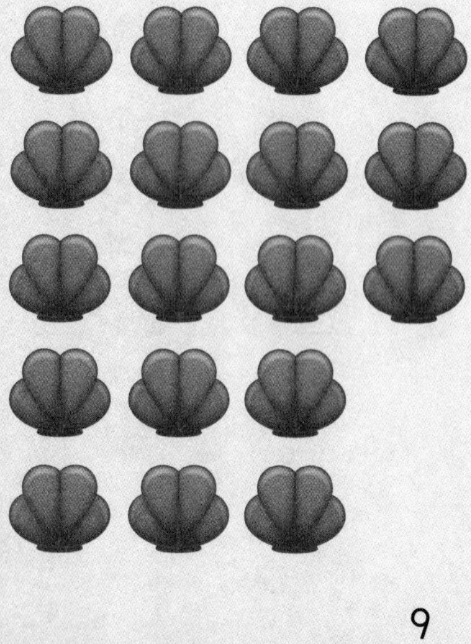

9

8

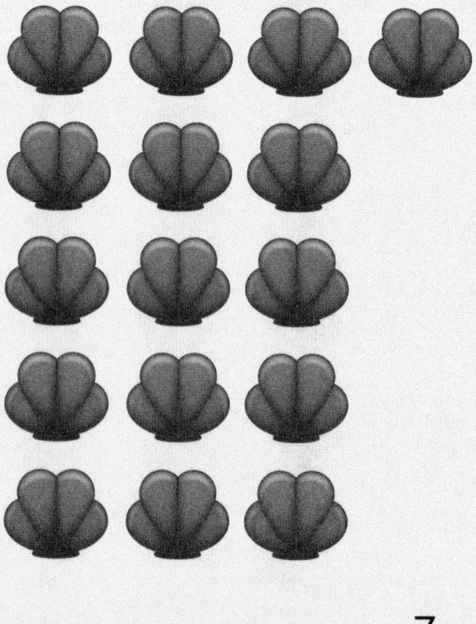

7

Cut out these flash cards. Use them to practise numbers and number words.

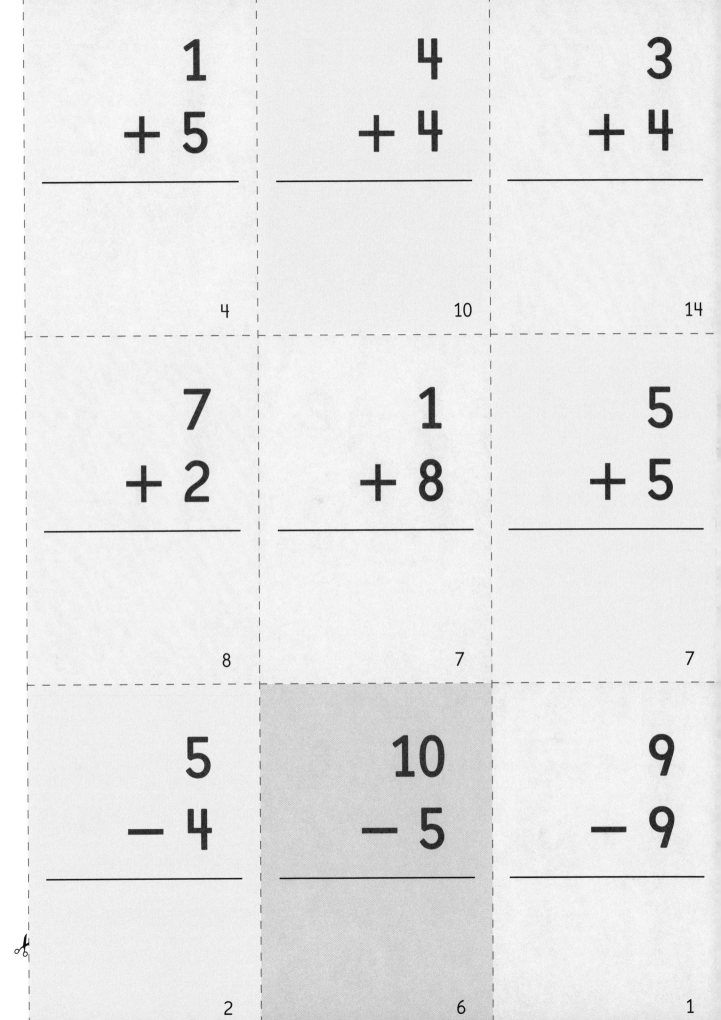

Cut out these flash cards. Use them to practise addition and subtraction.

$$\begin{array}{r} 1 \\ + 5 \\ \hline \end{array}$$

4

$$\begin{array}{r} 4 \\ + 4 \\ \hline \end{array}$$

10

$$\begin{array}{r} 3 \\ + 4 \\ \hline \end{array}$$

14

$$\begin{array}{r} 7 \\ + 2 \\ \hline \end{array}$$

8

$$\begin{array}{r} 1 \\ + 8 \\ \hline \end{array}$$

7

$$\begin{array}{r} 5 \\ + 5 \\ \hline \end{array}$$

7

$$\begin{array}{r} 5 \\ - 4 \\ \hline \end{array}$$

2

$$\begin{array}{r} 10 \\ - 5 \\ \hline \end{array}$$

6

$$\begin{array}{r} 9 \\ - 9 \\ \hline \end{array}$$

1

$$\begin{array}{r} 10 \\ + 4 \\ \hline \end{array}$$

7

$$\begin{array}{r} 3 \\ + 7 \\ \hline \end{array}$$

8

$$\begin{array}{r} 2 \\ + 2 \\ \hline \end{array}$$

6

$$\begin{array}{r} 6 \\ + 1 \\ \hline \end{array}$$

10

$$\begin{array}{r} 2 \\ + 5 \\ \hline \end{array}$$

9

$$\begin{array}{r} 6 \\ + 2 \\ \hline \end{array}$$

9

$$\begin{array}{r} 7 \\ - 6 \\ \hline \end{array}$$

0

$$\begin{array}{r} 8 \\ - 2 \\ \hline \end{array}$$

5

$$\begin{array}{r} 6 \\ - 4 \\ \hline \end{array}$$

1

Cut out these flash cards. Use them to practise addition and subtraction.

Congratulations

_____ !

Print your name.

You have finished the
Brain Boost learning path.
Way to go!